The Christian Girl's Guide to Change Inside & Out!

LEGACY PRESS®

The Christian Girl's Guide to Change Inside & Out!

Rebecca Park Totilo

Dedication:

This book is lovingly dedicated in honor of my mother, Mary Park
who clung to me during my own "roller coaster" years!

And, special thanks to my daughter, Rachel Abigail Park,
for her inspiration and help with this book. Your own recent experience
through puberty really helped these pages come alive.

THE CHRISTIAN GIRL'S GUIDE TO CHANGE: INSIDE AND OUT
©2007 by Rebecca Park Totilo
ISBN 10: 1-58411-086-4
ISBN 13: 978-1-58411-086-6
Legacy reorder#: LP48216
JUVENILE NONFICTION / Religion / Christianity / Christian Life

Legacy Press
P.O. Box 261129
San Diego, CA 92196

Cover and Interior Illustrator: Shelley Dieterichs

Scriptures are from the *Holy Bible: New International Version* (North
American Edition), ©1973, 1978, 1984 by the International Bible
Society. Used by permission of Zondervan Bible Publishers.

Printed in the United States of America

Table of Contents

Chapter 10: My Spirit: Soaring with God 177

Dear Christian Girlfriend:

I am so excited you have invited me to join you during this time in your life. It really is a celebration of change! Certain things will happen quickly, while other changes will seem almost invisible and take forever to make their debut (you know the ones I am talking about). Some days you will feel like you swallowed a handful of Mexican jumping beans with **BURSTS OF GROWTH AND ENERGY.** Other days, you may feel so tired, you will plop right down into a beanbag chair on the floor with arms and legs spread out. *The Christian Girls Guide to Change: Inside and Out* will help you understand and celebrate these new "welcome" changes to your body, soul, and spirit.

During what seems like a **ROLLER-COASTER** of emotions into womanhood, this easy-to-follow book will smooth the way by answering pressing questions you may have about physical changes such as menstruation, acne (which can sometimes feel like you're watching a horror movie), odd body shapes, and other personal issues you may face. This guide is filled with tips, how-to's, and quizzes that will help you discover fun ways to pamper the sudden mood swing, plus offer creative ways to handle stress and those "unavoidable" awkward situations, like that FIRST CRUSH. Later on, you can curb your munchies with easy-to-follow recipes for healthy snacks. You will even discover some new exercises to help you keep that new girlie figure.

SUPER-SIZE YOUR SELF-ESTEEM AND CONFIDENCE when you present your inner beauty to the rest of the world using the basic tips for hair and nail care within this book — all in a way that pleases God. And finally, you will soar with inspiration as you follow the simple suggestions in the "Head-to-Toe" tips, "Celebrating with God" devotions, and "Pampered by the Word" scriptures — while learning about your body and soul, and deepening your faith in our Creator.

Your New CGBFF,
Rebecca Park Totilo

Let the celebration begin!

Chapter One

Changes Inside and Out

Be happy while you are young,
and let your heart give you joy
in the days of your youth.

~Ecclesiastes 12:1

If My Body Had a MySpace Page

Here's what my profile would look like with all of the big changes that are taking place inside and out.

MYBODY.COM ✳

JUST THE FACTS:

Name: _Carly From Italy_

Age: _12_

Grade: _6th_

Weight: _____

Height: _____

Hair Color: _Brown_

MY SELF-PORTRAIT

CHANGES IN THE LAST YEAR

_____
_____
_____
_____
_____
_____
_____

WHAT I EXPECT AFTER ALL OF THESE CHANGES

_____
_____
_____

WHAT FRIENDS SAY ABOUT ME.... _Crazy_

Join the Body Language Chat Room Below!

✳ You're on the go, girl. You will (now or in the near future) climb in height. Your legs will lengthen and grooooooowwwww.

✳ Your emotions are a bit topsy-turvy. One minute you're crying, the next minute you're rolling in laughter.

✳ Your menstrual cycle (period) will start, if it hasn't already.

✳ You feel everyone staring at the huge zit on the tip of your nose (or at least you think they are).

✳ You have noticeable hair growing on your legs, underarms, and in other new places.

✳ You find yourself spending more time in the bathroom primping, in the refrigerator munching, and in the bed sleeping (lots more).

✳ You suddenly find the boy who lives next door to you isn't so creepy after all. In fact, you kinda think he's cute.

● ●

It is something that every girl will go through, is dealing with right now, or already has experienced. Somewhere between the ages of eight and thirteen years old, you will take a seat for the ride of your life — **PUBERTY!**

What's Puberty?

Puberty is when your body begins to change from being a little girl into a woman. Your body will grow and change its shape and size in all sorts of ways. You will see changes in your hair, skin, and other places in your body. This is because your pituitary gland (a pea-shaped organ located at the bottom of your brain) starts to produce very important hormones (special chemicals) that go to work on certain parts of your body. New hormones that are produced in a girl's body during puberty are called estrogen and progesterone. During this time, your body will change and grow faster than it has since you were a baby. With all this "growth spurt" stuff, it can seem like one part of your body, your legs for instance, are growing faster than any other part of your body. You may feel like the silly looking man that walks around on stilts.

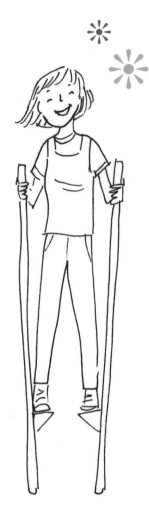

Are You Climbing the Wall to Change?

Like a rock-climbing wall, puberty is full of changes that you will experience or have already experienced. Each stage of the climb is exciting and challenging. To see where you are on the climb, circle those characteristics that apply to you.

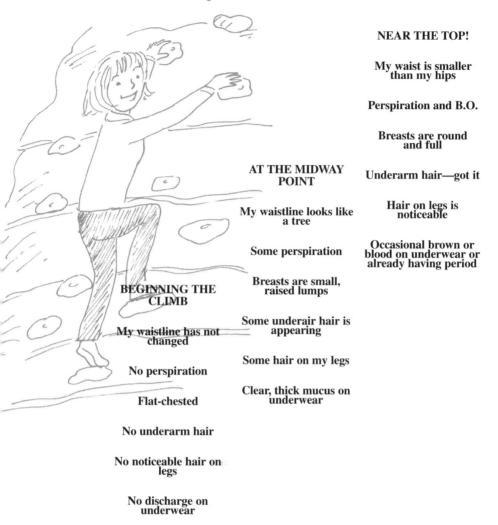

NEAR THE TOP!

My waist is smaller than my hips

Perspiration and B.O.

Breasts are round and full

Underarm hair—got it

Hair on legs is noticeable

Occasional brown or blood on underwear or already having period

AT THE MIDWAY POINT

My waistline looks like a tree

Some perspiration

Breasts are small, raised lumps

Some underair hair is appearing

Some hair on my legs

Clear, thick mucus on underwear

BEGINNING THE CLIMB

My waistline has not changed

No perspiration

Flat-chested

No underarm hair

No noticeable hair on legs

No discharge on underwear

If you are at the beginning of the climb, you haven't started puberty. And that's okay, because you will. You're smart to get prepared now for all the changes that lie ahead. Reading this guide will help you be ready when the time comes.

If you are at the midway point, you are now strapped in for this ride called puberty and are already experiencing growth spurts. Internal changes are taking place now, preparing you for womanhood. Hang on, you will get through all the ups and downs that it brings and hopefully this guide will help you understand everything that is going on inside you.

17

If you are near the top, things are in full swing for you and you are well on your way to becoming a woman. It seems that the worst part is over for you and now it is all down hill. Gradually, everything will become easier for you; this guide can help you answer some of the questions you may still have about puberty and help you adjust to the new you.

Celebrate the Change ·······················

This is a once-in-a-lifetime event for you. It is a time for celebration, now that you are becoming a woman. Pamper yourself by taking a long bubble bath or try one of these ideas below:

Have a "Spa" Party

You're the guest of honor for this party. It can be a private party — just you. Or, you can invite a couple of close friends over to share in your celebration at a sleepover. Who knows? Maybe they are experiencing some recent developments, too. For entertainment give each other manicures and facials, or make some stardust body glitter on page 20 and rainbow twirl lip gloss on page 171 in this book.

Start a Celebration Journal

Visit your local store for a blank journal and start keeping track of significant changes and developments in your body and soul. Write about your personal feelings, hopes, dreams, and fears. Someday you will be able to look back and see how much you have grown into a beautiful woman.

Plant an Herb Garden

Try growing some lemon, mint or lavender in a small pot and place in a kitchen window. You can use their fragrant leaves in some of the recipes contained in this book in place of essential oils. You can also use these fresh herbs to zest up an otherwise dull salad or meat dish or place in a small sachet bag to freshen up a sock drawer.

Shooooooooooopppppppppping!!!!

What girl doesn't like to shop? Ask Mom or Dad to take you to a nearby store so you can splurge on some new hair clips or a manicure set.

Mom and Daughter Ice Cream Outing

Just the two of you — it's a date. She will want to share this special moment with you. Besides, who can pass up the opportunity to indulge in a banana split covered in hot fudge or strawberry topping, whipped cream, nuts, and a cherry on top.

Make IT!  Stardust Body Glitter

Body glitter will add that touch of sparkle to your complexion and will moisturize your skin, too. This is an activity that is fun to do at a sleepover or for a spa-theme party with your best buddies.

What You Will Need:

✳ small bowl

✳ small plastic or glass container
(or clean, empty lip gloss container)

✳ 3 tablespoons un-medicated aloe vera gel (available at drug stores near sunscreen or lotion products)

✳ ½ teaspoon fine glitter (available at craft supply stores)

✳ 1 drop essential oil (available at craft supply stores or health food grocers)

What to Do:

1. In a small bowl, mix 3 tablespoons of aloe vera gel and ½ teaspoon of very fine glitter (any color of your choice) together.

2. If desired, add one drop of essential oil (any fragrance you like) and stir until blended.

3. Store at room temperature in a small plastic or jar container.

4. Use your body glitter for any special occasion to give you that extra sparkle.

For you created my inmost being,
knit me together in my mother's wo[mb]
praise you because I am fearfully an[d]
wonderfully made; your works are
wonderful, I know that full well.
Psalm 139:13 - 14

Celebrating with God Devotion:
Crystal Lil's Antique Shop

Marisa, Suzie, and Alexis climbed out of the SUV to follow Marisa's mom into Crystal Lil's antique shop. Marisa and her friends immediately began to explore each aisle filled with dusty relics from the past. Following one another, the three friends climbed a rickety staircase up to an attic. Old trunks filled with hats and frilly scarves lined the wall of peeling wallpaper. Alexis immediately grabbed a hat to try on. "Hey, look at me everyone!" Alexis shouted.

Each girl laughed as they tried on different color hats and scarves. Suzie made her way through the maze of furniture to find a mirror to see what she looked like. Near the back of the room, Suzie stepped in front of what appeared to be a normal full-length mirror. She looked at the reflection. The girl now standing in front of her was short and fat. For a moment she really believed what she saw.

"You guys! Come here!" Suzie called her friends over. "I told you guys I was fat. I need to lose weight. I hate how I look." She sadly dropped her gaze.

"You're not fat at all," Marisa stated. "It's the mirror. See?" Marisa stepped in front of the mirror to show how her shape changed.

"Look at the back, it's peeling and wavy." Alexis explained.

21

a's reflection. "I guess you're right. That old
ys, I suppose."

risa's mom downstairs, Alexis stopped her
ror made us look funny, but we really
ort or fat, it doesn't matter how we look on
made each of our bodies different and special. He
as beautiful."

✳ ✳ ✳ ✳ ✳ ✳ ✳ ✳ ✳ ✳ ✳ ✳ ✳ ✳ ✳ ✳ ✳ ✳ ✳
✳
✳
✳ *You may think that you're too short, or ugly and need to lose*
weight, but God doesn't see you that way. He made each of us
✳ *girls different — short or tall, stocky or lean. If we all looked*
✳ *the same, it would be a pretty dull world. God loves all of His*
✳ *creation, no matter how odd we think they look on the outside.*
✳ *The Bible tells us in the book of Genesis, God made male and*
✳ *female in His image and called it "very good." He is pleased*
✳ *with the different people He created — including you!*

✳ ✳ ✳ ✳ ✳ ✳ ✳ ✳ ✳ ✳ ✳ ✳ ✳ ✳ ✳ ✳ ✳ ✳ ✳

How Do I Shape Up?

One of God's most wonderful creations is the human body. It comes in
many various shapes and sizes. Just like a snowflake, no two are
exactly alike. If you have a full-length mirror, go stand in front of it.

✳ ✳ ✳ What do you see?

Let's be realistic. Not everyone is going to look like the supermodel
you see on magazine covers. Most of them don't even look that good
in real life, because the pictures have been "doctored" or touched up
to look perfect. Your mom, your teacher, and even your next door

neighbor — now these are what real women look like. And, God sees you as perfect, just the way he made you.

Try not to think, "I'm too fat" or "I'm thin as a rail." Instead, tell yourself, **"I aM fEaRfULLy aND WONDERfULLy MaDE."** That's how you are seen in God's eyes and that's the way He wants you to see yourself. And no matter what shape God blessed your body with, it is up to you to make the most with what you've got.

In Psalm 139:15-16 it says God made you in secret and knows your frame. This scripture refers to the frame that lies beneath your skin, called your skeleton. This is the framework for your body type. It is uniquely yours and will grow and develop into the shape God has predestined (with the help of your parents' genes). Your frame cannot be changed. If you are petite and short you may never be tall, just like your friend who has broad hips may never have narrow ones. It's the way God made each of us.

Pampered by The WORD

My frame was not hidden from you when I was made in the secret place...
Psalm 139:15

Body Shape Cutout Activity

Here's one way to figure out what body type you have. Wear your body suit or swimsuit for this activity.

What You Need:

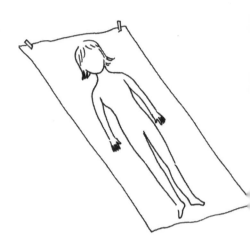

✳ body suit or swimsuit

✳ several sheets of newspaper

✳ scissors

✳ tape

✳ red or black marker

✳ someone to help

What to Do:

1. On the floor, unfold newspaper and lay several sheets flat (long ways). Tape ends together to create one long piece long enough for you to lie on.

2. In your body suit or swimsuit, lie down on the newspaper with arms and legs slightly spread apart.

3. Have your friend or helper trace around your body using the red or black marker.

4. Cut your shape out of the newspaper.

5. Grade your shape by checking off the similarities you have with the three body types described. The more checkmarks you have for one type, the more likely that is your body type.

6. Save your body shape for one year and see how your body changes.

Take a look to see where your body type fits into the three main groups. You may match all the descriptions in one category or you may be a combination of more than one.

Checklist for Body Type

No matter if you are thin, curvy, or something in between, what really counts is how you take care of yourself. Eating right and staying fit are two ways to make the most out of what God has given you. Don't let your particular type stop you from enjoying something you love to do such as swimming or ballet dancing. Even if your body isn't muscular, you still want to tone the muscles you do have.

☐ **Thin Body**
Type #1:

slender shape

narrow shoulders

long arms and legs

small breasts

flat stomach

☐ **Curvy Body**
Type #2:

soft, round figure

pear-shaped body

short neck

full breasts

well-defined waist

☐ **Athletic Body**
Type #3:

more athletic shape

well-defined muscles

narrow waist

broad shoulders and hips

strong and limber

Regardless of your shape and size, you can be at the top of your game in fitness and health and have lots of fun in the process.

Things are Beginning to Shape Up

One of the tell-tale signs that you are entering the "puberty zone" is when your breasts begin to bud. This usually begins to take place for a girl between the ages eight and thirteen years old. Some girls' breasts develop quickly, while others change and mature gradually. You may have a friend who has more developed breasts and she's only 11, whereas another older friend may be flat as a board. There just doesn't seem to be a set timetable for when these things will happen. God made girls to develop at different ages and at different rates.

A girl's breasts will reach maturity four to five years after she first begins to bud. Also, breast development happens in stages. During this

time, you will notice that one breast may be larger than the other or one nipple points up and the other one down. Don't worry, as time goes on, and with all of the changing you will doing things will balance themselves out sooner or later. But, no matter what size you have, big or small, it's the way God made you and they are a perfect fit for you.

Breast Development

Use the following example to see which stage of development you are in and to learn what will happen next.

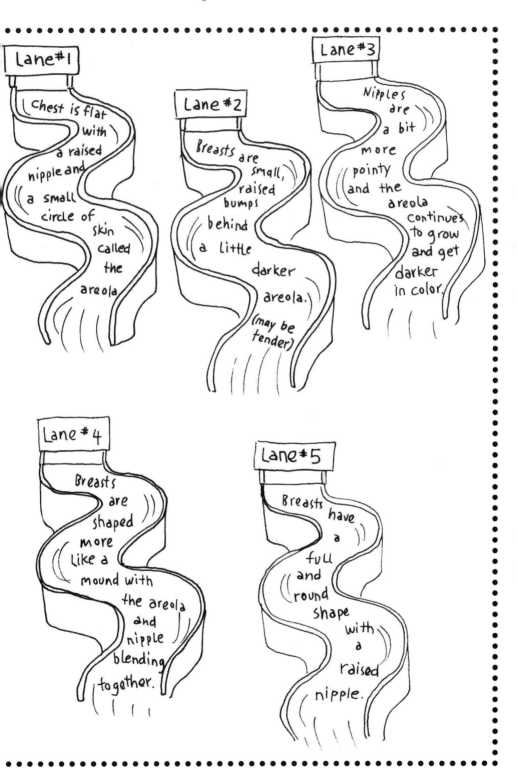

Lane #1

Chest is flat with a raised nipple and a small circle of skin called the areola

Lane #2

Breasts are small, raised bumps behind a little darker areola. (may be tender)

Lane #3

Nipples are a bit more pointy and the areola continues to grow and get darker in color.

Lane #4

Breasts are shaped more like a mound with the areola and nipple blending together.

Lane #5

Breasts have a full and round shape with a raised nipple.

How to Determine Your Correct Bra Size

Bra sizes come in two parts with a number and a letter like 32A, 34B, 36C and so on. The number is your chest size or measurement around your rib cage. The letter is your cup size or measurement around your breast. Here's how to figure out your size:

What You Will Need:

✳ tape measure

What To Do:

1. Wrap the measuring tape around your rib cage, just beneath your breasts.

2. Add 5 inches to your measurement, then round up to the nearest even number. This is your chest size.

3. Now, wrap the measuring tape across your chest over your nipples.

4. Subtract this measurement from your chest size. The difference is your cup measurement.

Use chart below to determine cup size.

DIFFERENCE	CUP SIZE
- 1	AAA
0	AA
1	A
2	B
3	C
4	D

5. Now, write down your bra size here _____. (Remember, Chest Size + Cup Size = Bra Size)

Of course, the best way to see if a bra fits is by trying it on before buying one. Here's a checklist to follow when purchasing one:

☐ **Does it feel comfortable and isn't riding up your back?** (It shouldn't be riding up your back or pinching you.)

☐ **Are the straps resting gently on shoulders and not digging in?** (These are usually adjustable, if necessary)

☐ **Does it look bumpy under your top?** If so, try another one that fits more snug and is smooth. (Basically, you don't want the bra to be distracting from your outer layer of clothing)

☐ **Is it adjustable?** (This will come in handy as you grow.)

InstaMssg Irene:
Breasts and Bras

Dear Irene:

I hate the fact that I barely have any breasts. It seems like if you don't have a big chest there is something wrong with you. I mean, just look at the way people dress and act on TV. What is all the fuss about?

Barely Annie

Dear Barely Annie:

You are right that large breasts do seem to get all the attention, but you should not feel bad that yours are small. There are some girls who have large breasts and are unhappy with them because boys stare at them. God made females in all shapes and sizes, but He didn't give women breasts just to look at. When a girl like your-self, grows up and has a baby, your breasts will provide the milk your baby needs. A mom's milk is the best food she can provide for her baby. And no matter what size breast you have, small or large, all sizes can provide milk for a baby.

Irene

Dear Irene:

I am 12 years old and just starting to notice some changes in my breasts. My mom says it is too soon for me to get a bra, but all my friends are getting one. Help! I don't want to feel left out.

Too Soon

Dear Too Soon:

One of the things you may want to do is try wearing a tank top or camisole under your blouse. This way others will not be able to tell if you are wearing a bra or not. After awhile, you can approach your mom again and explain that going without one makes you feel uncomfortable, especially if you feel like they are bouncing around when you are jogging or playing a sport. When you and your mom do go shopping together for a bra, you will find all sorts of bras for all different types of uses. For beginners, stores carry training bras, which will help you get used to wearing one. Then there are bras with an under-wire inside the cup to give extra support to girls who are larger. Soft-cup bras are for girls who are smaller in cup size and want comfort. Finally, a sports bra offers a snug fit for active girls. Not to worry. In no time you will be wearing one.

Irene

Clunker or Classic?

Just imagine: a few years from now you will be behind the wheel driving. What kind of car will it be? A sporty new convertible or Mom's minivan?

Have you ever seen an old car from the 1950's or 60's? Classic cars are still around because their owners take care of them. Upkeep and maintenance to keep cars in that "showroom" shape take a lot of work. A girl's body is an even more wonderful machine than a car. If you take care of yours, it will give you years of enjoyment. However, if you treat it as if it's nothing special — just a vehicle to get you where you want to go and you don't care how you treat it... hold on, it's going to be a bumpy ride.

Let's pretend you are that car. Are you going to be looking like a clunker years from now, or in "showroom" shape like a classic? Circle all the statements that apply to you. Afterwards, check your answers to see which vehicle you're driving.

I get outside as much as possible and enjoy the fresh air.

 I feel tired all the time and seldom get more than 6 hours of sleep.

 I shower daily.

 I seldom wash my hands before eating.

 I use sunscreen and wear a hat in the sun.

 Playing sports has always been a part of my life.

 I love any kind of aerobics that gets my heart beating fast.

 I hate gym class and avoid exercise whenever possible.

 My family says I am a couch potato.

 I will walk instead of catch a ride whenever possible.

 After climbing a flight of stairs, I am out of breath by the time I reach the top.

I have tried to exercise at home, but I have never stuck with it.

I regularly do stretching and warm ups before a practice or game.

I am a "hamburger and fries" kind of person.

Most of my diet consists of fried and/or greasy foods.

I love rice, beans, whole grain bread, and vegetables.

My hair frequently looks like an "oil slick."

I have scraggly nails and/or bite my nails.

I usually skip breakfast, or just eat doughnuts and pastries.

I will eat fresh vegetables like carrot sticks as a snack.

I skip meals if I'm too busy to eat.

My friends and I will share a comb or brush in the bathroom at school.

I drink milk instead of soda most of the time.

I rarely drink water.

I don't go to bed before 11pm.

If you circled mostly flat tires...

Oh no, look out...you might be headed for the junk yard. It's a good thing that you are reading this book for a tune-up in personal care, fitness and diet. If you follow the recommendations outlined in this guide you will be fully restored in no time.

If you circled mostly steering wheels...

You are behind the wheel in body care and fitness. Good for you! Keep reading this guide for more tips and advice on how to keep that showroom outlook on life. If your wheels just squeaked by on this quiz (barely made it), then follow the guidance offered on personal care and fitness and you will be on the road to looking and feeling great in no time.

InstaMssg Irene:
Slow Grower

Dear Irene:

My mom and I took a ride over to Shears Cuttery to get her hair cut and while I was waiting, I ran into an old school pal I hadn't seen since the 3rd grade. Wow, did she look all grown up! I felt so embarrassed because I still haven't...well, you know, developed in the chest area. My mom tells me all the time how much I've grown, but when I look in the mirror at myself, I don't see any change.

Samantha Slow Grower

Dear Samantha Slow Grower:

You shouldn't feel bad if your old schoolmate has grown up in some of the areas that you haven't developed in yet. It's not a contest, you know. God made every girl unique with her very own internal body clock for when changes are to take place. Some girls may get their period and start wearing bras at 11, and for others it may not happen until much later. Your time will come and before you know it you will see alarming changes. Keep in mind, when you plant seeds in the garden, they don't just pop up overnight. But beneath the surface changes are taking place and before you know it, you will be like a beautiful rose blooming into a beautiful woman. Our Creator knew what He was doing when He did this, so all of us could adjust to becoming a woman. It would be pretty tough to have to get used to all those changes overnight.

Irene

InstaMssg Irene:
Glamour Bods Magazine

Dear Irene:

I subscribe to *Glamour Bods* magazine. It's full of great fashion, beauty tips and secrets of the stars — many of which I have tried. In one beauty makeover article, they suggested using an avocado-egg yolk-mud paste to help clear acne — ugh! I tried it but it didn't help. How come I can't get my skin to look the way the model's complexion does on the magazine cover?

Glamour Bods Reader

Dear *Glamour Bods* Reader,

I'm going to let you in on another secret that they haven't shared with their readers. A secret that Victoria doesn't want you to know, nor anyone else in the fashion world for that matter: it's a smokescreen. Those images of beauty that you see on those magazines and inside those pages are not real. That flawless complexion with hair blowing in the breeze, attached to a killer body doesn't really exist. The truth of the matter is if you saw that same model on the street today, you'd probably not recognize that it is the same person. You see, magazines use several methods to create her artificial beauty, like heavy cosmetics to give her face that perfect complexion, a fan to give her hair that wind blown look, duct tape to hold her wardrobe in a way to draw attention to her chest, etc. Several professionals such as makeup artists, hairstylists, and wardrobe specialists help to create this perfect image. And if that weren't enough, after the photos are taken, computer graphic artists are called in to touch up the images by tucking a little here, take an inch off there. They "airbrush" to give her that perfect look, thus, the pictures have been altered electronically and no one knows differently. So you see, it isn't fair for you or any other girl to compare themselves to a fictitious character, is it? It's just not what God would want you to do. When God created Eve, He was pleased with His creation. He likes the way He made you, too. Just the way you are...imperfections and all.

Irene

Your Body Is God's House

Remember, your body is not just yours to do with as you please. The Bible calls your body a temple — the house or place where God resides. When girls like you and I accept Jesus in our hearts, He moves in and His Spirit lives in us. And, naturally, He will have to do some "furniture rearranging" in our hearts by dealing with attitudes or bad habits to help us rid our life of things that are harmful and don't belong there. He also wants to teach us new things about ourselves and how to take care of our bodies. He even warns us in Scripture that we must take care of His house or else! Wow, this body care business is serious stuff.

Don't you know that you yourselves are God's temple and that God's Spirit lives in you? If anyone destroys God's temple, God will destroy them; for God's temple is sacred, and you are that temple.

1 Corinthians 3:16-17

SO, WHAT'S A GIRL TO DO?

It's up to you now that you are getting older to take care of God's House. Things that your Mom used to do for you, like making sure you ate a healthy breakfast before school, washing and styling your hair, and getting you to bed so you'd get the right amount of sleep are things that you're going to have to start doing for yourself. Here's your chance to discover the real you.

Try This:

Do you ever feel **OVERWHELMED?** Write down your schedule here and see if there are any activities or things you need to cut out to give yourself more breaks.

Schedule

Chapter Two

Love Your Locks with Hair Care

Your hair is like royal tapestry;
the king is held captive by its tresses.
~Song of Songs 7:5

A CHRISTIAN GIRL LIKE YOU PROBABLY ALREADY KNOWS HOW IMPORTANT HAIR IS.

People can tell a lot about you by the way you wear your hair and if it is well-kept. They may see you as a neat and tidy kind of person because you keep your hair pinned up with barrettes. Or, they may think of you as a sports-buff kind of girl who wears a hair band and pony tail that is quick and easy and doesn't get in the way while you're in the game. Or, maybe they think that you don't concentrate much on your appearance because you wear it un-styled and down in your eyes. Yes, hair can say a lot about the kind of person you really are.

The Bible describes a woman's hair as her covering and calls it her "crown of glory."

That's because hair is symbolic of devotion to God. 1 Corinthians 11:15 says, "but that if a woman has long hair, it is her glory. For long hair is given to her as a covering." Apostle Paul's letter to the church at Corinth was addressing a very serious issue. You see, in Bible times women who served other gods and sold their bodies for money at pagan temples used to go around with shaven heads (or very short hair). He didn't want new believers to be like these awful women or even look like them. First impressions really do matter. He talked about a woman's hair as a sign of devotion to God because of a very special woman named Mary who wiped Jesus' feet with her long hair. It was a beautiful act of pure devotion to the Son of God.

Now, that doesn't mean you can't wear your hair in a cute bob. This Scripture means that a Christian girl needs to try not to model herself after the "worldly or unbelieving girls" who are trying to attract the wrong kind of attention with their hair or bodies.

Just like trying to part your hair straight down the middle, a Christian girl has to find balance in caring for her temple, but not allow her hair (or another part of her body) to become the most important thing in her life.

Hair Basics

What girl doesn't want her hair to be healthy and lustrous with lots of shine and bounce? It's easy once you know how. Like skin care, hair requires its own basic routine, with which you need to be consistent. It's a matter of nourishing, cleaning, and getting a great cut or style that you can manage.

Oil Check Activity

Before grabbing the shampoo and conditioner, it is important to identify the texture of your hair and its type (dry, oily, normal). Try this at home.

To figure out your hair type:

On the second day after washing your hair, dab a tissue (or toilet paper) on your scalp. If it has an oil blot, you have normal hair. If the tissue doesn't have anything on it, your hair is dry. If the strands of your hair stick to each other, then your hair is oily.

☀ Dry Hair

Dry hair can be caused by inactive oil glands or over-exposure to pool chemicals, sun, or harsh shampoos. Chemicals block pores, not allowing oil to flow on the surface.

Cure:

Dry hair needs plenty of nourishment. Massage with "hot oil" treatments at least once a week. Use mild shampoo and unplug the electric curlers, curling irons and blow dryers for awhile.

☀ Oily Hair

If you have oily skin, you probably have oily hair too. This is due to an over-secretion of oil and hair will look dirty even after shampooing.

Cure:

Wash your hair every other day or even more frequently, depending on your circumstances. Rinse with lemon juice. Use shampoos rich in henna. Avoid eating greasy foods and add more dark green vegetables to your diet.

☀ Normal Hair

This is the ideal hair type, with a good balance of oil and it doesn't look dried out. To keep hair in this condition, maintain a good diet and proper care.

Basic Hair Care Steps

✳ Shampooing

You will want to make sure you are using a shampoo that matches your hair type. Before starting, comb through with a wide-toothed comb to prevent tangles. Wet your hair and pour a quarter-sized amount of shampoo into your hands, then apply to your scalp. Massage your entire head firmly in rotating and circular movements. Do not scrub or over massage your scalp while washing. Rinse thoroughly with warm water. Apply more shampoo and massage for a second time if necessary. Dry hair gently by blotting hair dry with a towel (don't rub). Allow hair to dry naturally whenever possible. Ideally, try to wash your hair every other day to keep it clean and healthy. Switch shampoos once a month to avoid buildup.

✳ Conditioning

No matter what type of hair you have, your hair should be conditioned to keep it shiny (especially if you have dry hair). If you have oily hair, apply conditioner only on the ends of your hair. After shampooing, gently squeeze out excess water. Comb hair with your fingers or large-toothed comb from the roots to the ends to remove tangles. Rub conditioner through your hair (not your scalp) with your fingers and keep on your hair for 5 minutes. Massage hair to loosen conditioner and rinse with warm water. Allow hair to dry naturally.

※ Bad Hair Days

Are you frazzled with frizzes? It's not hard to reach hair heaven, once you know how. A good hair day means you have been able to tame the wild mane. A bad hair day is when you face one of these problems.

※ Dandruff

Dandruff is when you see small white flakes like snow on your shoulders. It is the excessive shedding of outermost skin cells. Causes for this can be poor blood circulation, improper diet, stress or from not rinsing well enough after shampooing. If this problem ails you, try using a medicated shampoo that treats this condition.

※ Split Ends

Split ends are caused from the use of heated appliances such as hair dryers and curling irons. Another cause may be from using hair color or the wrong type of brush. To keep hair in shape, try one or all of the following:

1. Trim hair every six weeks.

2. Use a conditioner on the ends of your hair.

3. Switch to a wide-toothed comb or brush with widely spaced bristles.

❋ Hair Loss

Don't worry, it's natural to lose about fifty to a hundred hairs a day. What's even more amazing is that God knows the exact number of them. One of the causes of hair loss is the daily repetition of pulling hair back tightly in a pony tail or using rubber bands, which can damage and break hair. Alternating hairstyles will prevent this.

❋ Hair In Other Places

As you continue to change, you will notice more hair sprouting in other places such as your underarms and on your legs. Before grabbing the razor, you will want to talk to your mom about  when you should start shaving. Once you and your mom agree you are ready, follow these simple steps to help you get started:

1. Wet legs or underarms.

2. Work up a good lather of shaving cream or gel, so you won't nick yourself.

3. Start at the bottom of your leg and pull the razor up in a gentle, firm stroke. For underarms, start at the top and use short strokes.

4. Rinse razor often, so it doesn't get clogged.

5. Store razor in a clean, dry place.

Head-To-Toe Tip

For Healthy, Shiny Hair

1. Wash your hair every other day. Massaging your scalp will stimulate oil glands to add sheen to your hair.

2. Use a shampoo that is specially designed for your hair type (dry, oily, combination) and always rinse with cool or warm clean water. No time for a shower? Try using a dry shampoo like cornstarch. Sprinkle in your hair, let it absorb for a few minutes, then brush out. Great for when you are in a hurry!

3. Avoid using electric hair dryers or hot curling irons too often and allow your hair to dry naturally.

4. Always use a wide-toothed comb on wet hair. Using a brush can stretch and pull your hair causing it to break off leaving you with split ends.

5. Brush your hair each night about a hundred strokes before bed. This will remove dirt while increasing circulation and help spread the natural oils from your scalp throughout your hair. The best way is to bend forward at the waist, head down, brushing your hair back to front.

6. Use natural and organic hair products whenever possible and avoid those that contain chemicals since these will eventually damage your hair.

7. For dull, lifeless hair caused by a build-up of shampoos and conditioners try using a solution of plain apple-cider vinegar and water after regular shampooing. Rinse your hair with this solution (half and half mixture), then rinse out. Apply conditioner as usual afterwards. This can be done every two weeks if necessary.

8. To add a bit of highlight, rinse your just-washed hair with chamomile tea (brewed in hot water, then cooled) and/or lemon juice. Sit outside and let the sun do the rest.

9. For strawberry highlights, rinse your just-washed hair with brewed Red Zinger tea (available at health food stores) and/or lemon juice. Sit in the sunshine and dry naturally outdoors.

10. Visit your hair salon regularly for trims and/or cuts. This way you can keep split or dead ends in check and will help new hair grow faster.

11. For long hair, only condition the bottom half. Moisturizing the roots might give you a greasy look.

12. Don't wear headbands with teeth. These can cause hair breakage around your forehead. This goes for butterfly clips, metal clips, and rubber bands, too.

13. Only use about a nickel-sized dollop of styling gel, curl enhancer, or straightening balm. For mousse use only a golf ball-sized amount. Too much can make your hair look like you hit an oil-slick.

14. Frizzy hair tangles can be a problem for some. Try putting down the hot flat iron and towel-dry your hair. Then, add an alcohol-free taming gel or leave-in conditioner to tame the wild look.

15. Big hair not your thing? Sometimes static electricity can get in between your strands causing it to pouf up. Avoid using hair products

with alcohol, which add volume. To add moisture to your hair, apply equal parts of honey and shampoo once a week.

✳ Bungee Cord Hair Activity

Here are a couple of tests to try and see if your hair is healthy or not.

Test #1: Pull on a strand of hair without pulling it out of your scalp. Does it snap in half or does it stretch without returning to its original length? If so, it's damaged (maybe sun bleached or pool chemicals) and needs some intensive care.

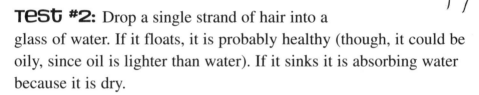

Test #2: Drop a single strand of hair into a glass of water. If it floats, it is probably healthy (though, it could be oily, since oil is lighter than water). If it sinks it is absorbing water because it is dry.

Test #3: Try threading (if it is straight) a strand of hair through a needle. If it glides in, it is in good condition. If not, then it may be damaged.

InstaMssg Irene:
Hairy Legs

Dear Irene:

I am embarrassed about the hair on my legs. I mean, it's blonde and everything, but there's lots of it. I asked my mom if I could start shaving and she said, "N-O!" Help!

Hairriet Leggetts

Dear Hairriet Leggetts:

You were right to check in with Mom first. Shaving your legs is something that will have to be done on a regular basis once you start (in other words: the rest of your life). The blonde hairs on your legs will begin to come in darker and coarser once you start shaving. Your mom may not think you are ready to start a shaving routine right now. I wouldn't worry too much about it. Your hair is fair and probably isn't noticeable to anyone else besides you.

Irene

Make IT! Fresh-Squeezed Lemon Rinse

To give your hair that finishing touch with summer highlights, try this rinse after shampooing your hair. Be sure and let it run down all the way from your scalp to your ends of your hair. Let the sun do the rest.

What You Will Need:

✳ glass
✳ 1 lemon
✳ 2 cups warm water

What To Do:

1. Mix the water and squeeze juice from the lemon in a glass.

2. Pour over your head, covering your hair after shampooing and conditioning as a final rinse.

3. Sit in sun to allow your hair to dry naturally.

Pampered by The WORD

And even the very hairs of your head are all numbered. Matthew 10:30

Try This:

Do you ever feel like pulling your hair out when you are angry? Do you beat your pillow? **STOMP YOUR FEET OR JUMP UP AND DOWN?** Describe how you let off steam. Now, list three people you can go to when you need to talk to someone about the way you feel.

1.

2.

3.

Polish Your Act with Nail Care

Who may ascend the hill of the Lord?
Who may stand in his holy place?
He who has clean hands and a pure heart. . .

~Psalm 24:3-4

A GOOD MANICURE IS A BASIC INGREDIENT TO THE PACKAGE FOR LOOKING GOOD... just like having healthy skin and a neat hairstyle. No matter whether your nails are long and polished with a hip new color or simply shaped and buffed, a girl with well-cared-for hands will look and feel more confident.

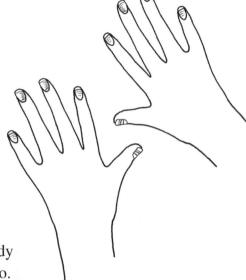

Believe it or not, one of the first things people look at when they meet you, besides your face, is your hands. Even when you're wearing your hair in the latest style or look fabulous in those to-die-for jeans, top celebrity nail-care experts agree: If your nails are not done, you're not done. And the truth is, it is probably the one place on your body you see the majority of the time too.

Maybe it's time to do something with those scraggly nails. Check out these next set of digits to see if the finger (or fingers) are pointing at you.

 **Do Your Hands Rank a Perfect 10?**

See how many of these fingers are pointing at you, then check out the insider secrets every girl should know for a stunning set of ten.

Left Hand:

A. Hangnails dangling in the breeze?

B. Brittle, dry nails?

C. Small, white bands?

D. Redness, dry and cracking?

E. Blisters?

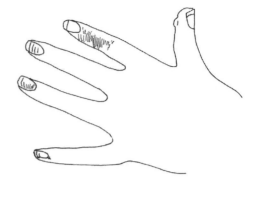

Right Hand:

F. Warts?

G. Short and never seem to grow?

H. Paper cuts?

I. Dirt under nails and grubby?

J. Calluses and dead skin?

Insider Solutions That Will Keep You Pointed In the Right Direction:

A. Keep these trimmed with nail clippers, especially if you are a nail biter. Never rip or tear out.

B. Brittle nails? Drink lots of water (especially in the winter months) and take a multi-vitamin or vitamin E to strengthen nails.

C. You are what you eat, and healthy-looking nails and hands are a direct result of proper nutrition. Small, white bands are a common indication of a protein-deficient diet.

Add more good sources of protein to your diet such as eggs, fish, meat, poultry, and legumes.

D. Redness and cracking are caused by dryness. Try using some hand lotion on your hands after washing them to keep them moisturized.

E. Blisters are soft worn patches of skin that are caused by the friction of rubbing, like when you rake your yard. The skin forms a bubble of fluid and sometimes pops. Wear a band-aid to protect it, until your skin heals.

F. Warts are harmless, yet ugly to look at. These small white bumps are caused by a virus that grows on people's hands and feet. Try applying a drop or two of frankincense essential oil to each wart every day. Typically, warts can take up to two or three months to go away using over-the-counter medications sold in drugstores. If you are in a hurry, ask a parent to take you to a dermatologist to have them removed.

G. Never seem to grow? Try rubbing your fingernails on one hand across the other hand, with a quick, rapid motion as if you were buffing them for five minutes. This stimulates the blood in your nail bed and will encourage growth. Do this three times a day and watch them grow.

H. Painful paper cut? Try blow-drying the cut, then dab a little aloe or vitamin E on for healing benefits.

I. Try using a nail brush to clean nails and be sure to wash your hands frequently to prevent illnesses, especially after you use the rest room and before you eat. For extra protection against germs, carry a small bottle of hand sanitizer (requires no water) to use when you are in a place where you can't wash your hands.

J. Calluses are tough, worn patches of skin, which sometimes form on the bottom of your feet. These can be removed by using a pumice stone. To prevent calluses on hands, try wearing gloves while working. To prevent calluses on feet, wear cotton socks.

Nail Down the Basics with These Tools

SOFT TOWEL –
Great for protecting the surface you are working on and for drying hands.

BOWL OF WARM WATER –
For loosening dirt under your nails and softening cuticles.

NAIL POLISH – The possibilities are endless. Here's where you can make a personal statement about your style or faith. Add a cross or heart to show others what you believe.

ORANGE STICK (or popsicle stick) – For gently pushing back cuticles around the nail bed.

NAIL POLISH REMOVER – A must for clean-up. Use non-acetone remover if you have sensitive skin.

COTTON BALLS – Only 100% cotton will do, if you don't want to leave fibers lingering around to get stuck in your wet polish.

CUTICLE SOFTENER – Great for softening cuticles so you can push them back.

EMERY BOARD – This file has two sides. The rough side is for shortening lengths and the fine side is for smoothing edges.

NAIL BRUSH – Extra soft, please! An old toothbrush also works well for getting dirt out from under the nail tips.

MOISTURIZER – Hand cream is the one thing you shouldn't scrimp on. Your hands are screaming "moisture please!"

EXTRA, EXTRA – You may also want to have on hand:

Pumice stone - Smoothes and removes rough calluses and dead skin.

Toe spacer - Keeps toes in place while paint is drying.

Home Salon Manicure

You don't have to go to a sophisticated salon for that polished look.
You can do-it-yourself as your own home manicurist.

What You Will Need:

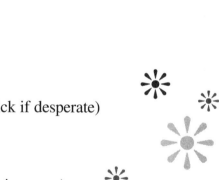

❋ hand towel

❋ warm water

❋ small bowl

❋ nail clippers

❋ nail brush

❋ nail polish

❋ nail polisher remover

❋ cotton pads (or balls)

❋ orange stick (or use a popsicle stick if desperate)

❋ emery board

❋ cuticle cream

❋ mild facial cleanser (or moisturizing soap)

❋ moisturizing hand lotion

❋ 2 Tablespoons olive oil

What To Do:

1. Remove old nail polish by wetting a cotton pad and holding on nails for a few seconds, allowing nail polish to dissolve. Then, wipe away in an outward sweeping motion to keep cuticles and skin clean.

2. Wash your hands with moisturizing soap and warm water. Pat hands dry with your hand towel.

3. Clip nails to a length slightly longer than what you want (mid to short length is ideal).

4. File with emery board to get nails to desired length. File from the outer corners toward the tip. Do not use a "sawing" motion (back and forth) — this will cause nails to become jagged.

5. In a small bowl, add 2 tablespoons of olive oil to warm water and soak hands in it for 5-10 minutes.

6. Clean nails with a nail brush; then apply cuticle cream to the cuticles. Massage hands with moisturizing hand lotion, using your thumb in a circular motion.

7. Using your orange stick, gently push back cuticles. Then, wipe hands again using your hand towel to remove excess lotion.

8. Take your nail polish and apply at the center of the nail with one stroke. Then, apply two more strokes on either side to cover nail. Be careful to only have enough polish on the brush for one stroke at a time. Allow 1-2 minutes to dry before applying a second coat.

9. Allow nails to dry completely before going on to other things. To speed up drying time, dip fingers into a bowl of icy water for a couple of minutes after your final coat. Air dry.

For added fun:

Use craft paints and a toothpick to add colorful designs to your nails.

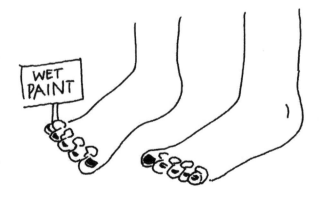

Pampered by The WORD

In her hand she holds the distaff and grasps the spindle with her fingers. She opens her arms to the poor and extends her hands to the needy.

Proverbs 31:19 - 20

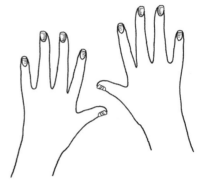

Head-To-Toe Tip

Clean & Smooth Techniques for Nails

❋ Try using a buffer for that natural shine as an alternative to nail polish.

❋ If nails become yellowed from polish, try using a little lemon juice or white vinegar to remove stains.

❋ For a quick fix to chipped polish, file the raised edges of the chip then add a coat of polish.

❋ Still don't have the knack for finger painting (your nails, that is)? Try using a light color polish that hides major goofs.

✳ When polishing nails, be careful not to sit under direct light, such as a lamp. This will cause polish to bubble. (Avoid fans and heaters, as these will cause bubbling too.)

✳ Don't share nail tools such as clippers with other family members. To prevent the spread of infection, soak clippers in rubbing alcohol for several minutes.

Tippee-Toe Top Shape

POOR, POOR, Pitiful feet...

They just don't seem to get any respect. You slip your shoes on and out the door you go never giving them a second thought. But, wait a minute. Aren't they the ones CaRRYiNG aLL tHe WeiGHt around here? Where would you be WitHOUt tHeM?

It's especially important that you keep them in tip-top shape since they will be taKiNG a POUNDiNG from you for the rest of your life.

Feet and legs have little or no oil glands so you will need to moisturize twice as often as you do for your hands. The best time to do this is after a bath for faster absorption.

For warmer weather when toes are exposed, you will want to give yourself a weekly pedicure.

Follow the same directions as for the Home Salon Manicure, but include these exceptions:

❋ Use toenail clippers to clip nails straight across.

❋ Use your emery board to smooth rough edges.

❋ Use your toe spacer to keep toes apart, to prevent smudging your polish. (Or, stuff cotton balls between each toe.)

❋ Try adventurous nail polish colors here. (No one will see them when you're wearing your sneakers.)

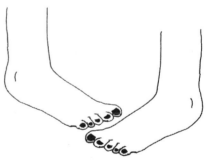

Stinky Feet

To avoid **foot troubles** like **odor,** always wear clean cotton socks when wearing closed-toe shoes. Socks will help absorb sweat. To deodorize your shoes, try sprinkling a little baking soda inside them and leave until next use. Shake out excess powder before wearing.

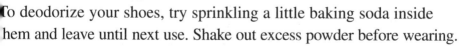

 Itchy Feet

ATHLETE'S FOOT is a fungus
people get from walking around
barefoot, especially at pools and
health spas. You can avoid catching
this by wearing flip-flops at the pool
or shower shoes while changing in
the gym. If you do notice you suddenly have itchy toes or the skin on
the bottom of your feet is cracking,
there are over-the-counter medicines
you can use to treat it.

 Just the Feet, Pete

No one knows for sure whether pedicures were in style during Bible
times, but the Scriptures do mention **FOOT WASHING.** In ancient
times, when a visitor came into a house, they took off their sandals
and a good host offered to wash their guest's dusty feet. Judging by
the
discussion between Jesus' disciples in John 13, it was considered one
of the least desirable jobs. Jesus decided to do it for them as a way of
showing them how to be humble. For the Christian girl today, this may
not mean literally washing another's feet (it could, though), but instead
doing an unpleasant chore for someone at home, like scrubbing out the
trash can or cleaning the toilet, etc. Think about ways you can
"WASH ONE ANOTHER'S FEET" this week.

✳ ✳ ✳ ✳ ✳ ✳ ✳ ✳ ✳ ✳ ✳ ✳ ✳ ✳ ✳

 **Make IT!**

Treat For the Feet

Here's a way you can show your feet appreciation for all they do for you. Try this soak and give your toes a break.

What You Will Need:

✳ towel

✳ basin (large enough to hold your feet)

✳ ¼ cup Epsom salts (available   at grocery or drug store)

✳ warm water

✳ 3 herbal mint tea bags

What to Do:

1. Spread a towel on the floor in front of the chair where you will soak.

2. Pour Epsom salts into the basin and fill with warm water, until it reaches ankle height.

3. Drop tea bags into the basin.

4. Soak feet for 5-10 minutes, then rinse and dry.

Enjoy

Try This:

Draw a picture of what you look like when you feel exhausted. What do you do to get back on your feet?

Sugar Scrub

Don't be tempted to eat this one. It exfoliates dead skin cells from your feet leaving your skin incredibly soft.

What You Will Need:

- ✳ mixing bowl
- ✳ 1 cup white sugar
- ✳ 1 cup avocado oil (acceptable substitute: vegetable glycerin)
- ✳ small amount of aloe vera gel
- ✳ 2 drops of lavender essential oil (optional)
- ✳ 2 drops of orange essential oil (optional)

Aloe Vera Gel

What To Do:

1. In a large mixing bowl, combine all ingredients.
2. Scoop some of the sugar scrub into your hands and massage gently onto your skin for one minute. You will begin to feel your skin tighten like a mask.

3. Leave on for five minutes before rinsing. You will want to use this on other parts of your body as well.

4. Some redness or blotches may develop after cleansing your skin. This is normal because of it being cleaned so well. You will not want to try this recipe out for the first time just hours before an important event like a school play or prom (especially if you use it on your face).

Pampered by The WORD

How beautiful on the mountains are the feet of those who bring good news, who proclaim peace, who bring good tidings, who proclaim salvation, who say to Zion, "Your God reigns!"

Isaiah 52:7

InstaMssg Irene:
Nail Biting Suspense

Dear Irene:

My nails are really gross. I can't help myself; I just chew away, especially when I am watching TV. I am not sure why I bite my nails, but I just can't seem to stop myself. Any suggestions on how to quit?

Nail Biter

Dear Nail Biter:

Ugly nails are nothing to laugh at.
Nail biting is a nervous habit caused by
stress, worry, or nervousness. You men-
tioned you did it while watching TV.
Are you watching suspenseful pro-
grams that are scary or have lots of
action in them? Maybe you should
consider doing something else with you
time like playing the piano or writing
in your journal? Of course, there may
be other causes for your worry or nervousness, which you will
want to explore to see what causes you to be upset. Pray and
ask God to help you not to fret or worry and to give you the
will-power to give up nail biting. In the meantime, here is one
way you can try to kick the nail biting habit. Pick a finger (start
with your pinky) and don't bite that nail for a week. You are free
to chew on the other nine. Leave this one to grow out. Then in the
following week, don't chew on the pinky or the ring finger. Feel
free to continue bite the other eight nails. Continue to do this
week after week until all your nails are grown out. Soon, you will
enjoy long nails and will want to pull out the polish and shine
them up. If all else fails, there is always a bitter flavored nail
polish at your local drugstore to discourage nail biting.

Irene

Chapter Four

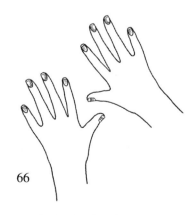

Facing the Horrors of Skin Care

. . .show me your face, let me hear your voice;
for your voice is sweet, and your face is lovely.

~Song of Songs 2:14

DEaLING WiTH aCNe DOeSN'T HaVe To Be SCaRY!

Zits (also called pimples) are probably one of the most dreaded parts of puberty. But, hold on. This book is going to show you how to get your complexion in shape and keep your skin healthy and blemish free. Creepy skin problems won't keep you hiding in the dark anymore.

What Is Your Skin Type?

It's important to know before starting any skin care regime what type of skin you have so you will know what kind of cleaners and moisturizers to use. Take this skin test to find out your type.

What You Will Need:

✳ lens cleaning tissue paper or rice paper

What To Do:

First, wash your face and pat it dry. Take several lens papers and pat each one on different parts of your face. If your skin is oily, the lens paper will stick to your face and leave an oil spot on the paper (or make it look translucent). If the paper doesn't stick or pick

up any oil, then your skin is dry. If the lens paper sticks only in the "T-zone" area of your face (forehead, nose and chin), then you have combination or normal skin.

Skin Types

OiLY

If you have oily skin, your complexion tends to be shiny. Your pores are larger and are prone to blackheads and pimples.

COMBiNation/NORMaL

If you have a smooth and even texture with medium pores, your skin is normal. You may have some dryness on the cheeks and experience oil in the T-zone.

SENSitive

If you blush easily and tend to break out with rash or allergies, your skin is sensitive. Your pores are small and delicate.

DRY

If your skin feels tight, especially after washing it, you have dry skin. Your skin may flake, seem dull, and have red patches or blotches on it.

Daily Skin Care

Dead skin cells, perspiration and grime from the atmosphere clog your pores, giving your skin a dull and lifeless appearance. Here's a daily care regimen that takes only minutes a day and will breathe life back into your complexion in no time flat. And, if you select quality skin care products that match

your skin type, performing this simple regimen will produce almost immediate, visible results.

✳ Step One:

steam: Before going to bed, soak a washcloth in steamy, hot water and wring lightly. Hold close to your face for 2 minutes. The steam will open your pores.

✳ Step Two:

Cleanse: While your pores are open, splash warm water on your face and neck. Pour a workable amount of facial cleanser into your hands and rub together until it lathers. Using your fingertips (or facial brush), delicately massage into your skin in a circular motion for about 30 seconds. Avoid using harsh hand soap.

✳ Step Three:

Tone: Using a cotton ball, dampen with toner (alcohol-free) and gently wipe your entire face and neck area.

✳ Step Four:

Moisturize: Apply a small amount of moisturizer into your hands and work into your skin in an upward, circular motion. Try not to use too much. In order for moisturizer to work and protect your skin, it needs to be applied to a clean face.

Keep in mind that your daily skin care program will only help if it's done on a regular basis. Cleansers won't get your face clean if they are left in the container. To ensure a radiant complexion, you may want to exfoliate occasionally to remove dead cells and encourage new cell growth and give your skin that healthy glow.

Acne and Pimples and Zits, OH MY!

Pimples, blemishes, zits, whiteheads, blackheads or just an all-in-all **BREAKOUT.** It is known by many names, but whatever you want to call it, it is acne. During puberty, your body produces excessive oil due to hormones. When your pores become clogged with oil, dirt, and dead skin cells, **ACNE HaPPeNS!**

Why ME?

Are you troubled by acne? **YOU'Re NOt aLONe.** Acne is the most common skin condition in the United States and over 85% of the population at some point has had to deal with it. Any girl who has had it, or is dealing with it knows how stressful it can be. However, with careful skin care, you can keep acne under control.

Pimple Popping Myths

Test your skin care savvy by answering "T" for true and "F" for false to see if you can clear up the confusion of acne.

T or F   1. Eating fast food like French fries causes breakouts.

T or F   2. Getting a tan will help clear up acne.

T or F   3. You should wash your face more often than usual, like 3 or 4 times a day.

T or F   4. When washing your face you should use an astringent or toner to dry up pimples.

T or F   5. All sun screens and moisturizers should be avoided.

T or F   6. The black stuff inside blackheads is dirt.

T or F   7. You should let acne run its course and not treat it.

T or F   8. Everyone eventually outgrows acne.

T or F   9. Wearing makeup is an absolute no-no.

T or F   10. Using hair spray and styling gels will not affect your acne.

Check your answers below:

1. **False.** Doctors say there is no evidence that fried foods affect the skin. Now, if you find yourself breaking out more often after eating certain foods, it makes sense to avoid and eliminate these from your diet until your skin clears up. Needless to say, it doesn't hurt to maintain a healthy, well-balanced diet.

2. **False.** Tanning will temporarily help dry up the oils in your skin, but it is only a short term benefit. Going in the sun with your skin unprotected can cause premature aging and skin damage.

3. **False.** Washing your face more often than normal will not help and, in fact, will cause more problems. Using harsh scrubs can inflame your existing acne.

4. **False.** Astringents or toners with alcohol may be too harsh for your skin. These will cause irritation and dryness.

5. **False.** Wearing a sunscreen or moisturizer with SPF of 15 or higher will help protect your skin from sun damage.

6. **False.** Unfortunately, the black stuff is not dirt and cannot be scrubbed away. Doctors believe it is a combination of oil and dead skin cells. A blackhead is a clogged pore that is open at the skin's surface; oxygen turns the material inside darker.

7. **False.** Acne is a treatable condition and there is no reason to wait for skin to clear up. The longer you wait for it to clear up, the greater the risk is for permanent scarring.

8. **False.** Adults can also suffer from acne later in life.

9. **False.** It is fine to wear a foundation that doesn't clog pores and is oil-free.

10. **False.** Hair products that contain oil and/or alcohol can cause irritation to your skin when your hair rubs your skin.

Hitting the Target:

If you got less than 5 questions right...

You need to work on your skin care routine and learn the proper way to care for your skin. What you have been doing may be causing you more harm than good. Wash, don't scrub your face, wear sunscreen, and take a look at the products you are using on your face and hair — they may need replacing.

If you got 5 to 7 questions right...

You're off to a good start, but could do more to get your skin through this tough time. Wash your face with a mild cleanser, wear sunscreen while out in the sun, and choose products that will not cause more problems for you, such as oil-free, clog-free, and formulated for people with acne.

If you got 8 or more questions right...

Way to go! You know what your skin needs and are giving it the special care it needs. Make sure to stick with your skin-care regimen daily.

Acne 101

✳ Stick with your skin care regime. Washing your face twice a day will help prevent blemishes from getting out of hand.

✳ Don't pop pimples. The oils and dirt on your hands can cause more trouble for you. Plus, picking at them can lead to scarring.

✳ Try an over-the-counter medication from the drugstore for mild cases. If your skin doesn't seem to respond to these products in a month or so, ask your mom about taking you to a dermatologist for treatment.

Try This:

Describe a time when you felt **SHY** because of the way you looked. How did God help you through it?

Head-To-Toe Tip

Tips for a Glowing Complexion

✳ Drink 8 glasses of water everyday.

✳ Eat a healthy diet rich in fresh fruits and vegetables.

✳ Get a good night's sleep.

✳ Take a multi-vitamin to ensure your body gets what it needs.

✳ Practice a daily skin care routine and cleanse no more than twice a day.

✳ Know your skin type and what products work for you.

✳ Stay fit by exercising regularly.

✳ Limit your intake of sodas with caffeine.

✳ Avoid excessive exposure to harsh weather and too much time in the sun.

InstaMssg Irene:
Chocolate and Acne

Dear Irene:

I have heard that chocolate can cause acne. Is that true? I sure hope not, because I love candy.

Candie

Dear Candie:

You will be relieved to know that sugary sweets like chocolate don't cause acne or affect the skin in this way. Some people may have believed this at one time because they developed an allergy or sensitivity to it. Many people are sensitive to certain foods like shellfish and sushi as well and breakout with pimples. You will need to watch and see if this happens to you. In the meantime, enjoy your sweets in moderation and give your skin a boost with a healthy diet.

InstaMssg Irene:

Body Tattoos

Dear Irene:

A friend of mine has a long stem rose tattoo on her pinky. I think it is so cool. I want one, but my mom said, "NO WAY." Is there any way to convince her it is okay?

Tatty Too

Dear Tatty Too:

Your mom may believe that it's wrong because of what the Bible says about this practice. In Leviticus 19:28 it says, "Do not cut your bodies for the dead or put tattoo marks on yourselves. I am the LORD." God gave this instruction to Moses and the people of Israel because other cultures who worshiped the sun god Baal would mark their bodies with magical symbols on their hands and foreheads.

Today the custom of marking a person's body with a tattoo isn't necessarily attached to a person's belief and it has become a popular fad. Your mom may think that having a tattoo on your temple is like graffiti on a wall and that it trashes your temple. The best thing to do is honor your mom with obedience and only be marked (invisibly) and sealed with the Holy Spirit.

Make IT!

Irene

Green Facial Mask

Facial masks are a wonderful way to make your skin glow and even out its tone. Here's one you can make yourself using all-natural ingredients for that "salon spa" experience. If you have an oily complexion, use this recipe for a deep cleansing once a week for a month.

What You Will Need:

✳ 2 small bowls

✳ 3 Tablespoons green clay (substitute white or pink clays if you have sensitive or dry skin — all are available at your local health food store)

✳ 2 drops rosemary essential oil

✳ 2 drops lemon essential oil

✳ 2 drops lavender essential oil

✳ 2 drops almond oil (or substitute another kind vegetable oil)

✳ 2 slices of fresh cucumber, peeled

What To Do:

1. Be sure and cleanse your face thoroughly with a mild liquid cleanser before applying any facial mask.

2. In a bowl, combine green clay, rosemary and lemon oils. Apply clay mixture evenly on face and neck.

3. Lay back and place one cucumber slice over each eye and relax.

4. Leave face mask on for 10 minutes. Rinse with warm water. Pat dry.

5. In another bowl, mix ¼ cup of vegetable oil and lavender oil.

6. For the finishing touch, apply to face for shine and moisturizing. Your face will glow.

As water reflects a face, so a man's heart reflects the man.

Proverbs 27:19

Chapter Five

The Merry-Go-Round of Menstruation

When a woman has her regular flow of blood,
the impurity of her monthly period will last seven days. . .
~Leviticus 15:19

SOME TIME DURING PUBERTY, YOU WILL GET YOUR FIRST MENSTRUAL PERIOD. This will be one of the biggest changes you will go through and may feel like you just stepped onto a carousel with all the ups and downs you will experience with it. Once you do start your monthly cycle, you will have a menstruation period every month until your late 40's or 50's.

When Will IT Start?

Every girl's body is different, so no one can say exactly when you will get your period. Most girls generally start around 1 ½ to 2 years after their breasts start to develop. A good sign you are getting close to starting your first period is when you see a thick, white mucous discharge on your underwear. This may happen for several months before your first period starts. Once you start your period, it means your body is now able to have a baby (of course, you will want to wait until you're married). If you haven't started your period yet, there is no rush. Your body still has some growing to do.

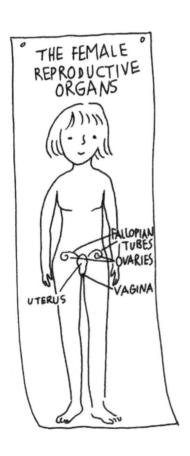

What's Happening Inside Your Body

Your body has two ovaries filled with thousands of tiny eggs and two fallopian tubes that connect the ovaries to the uterus or womb where babies grow. Each month one egg matures and pops out of the ovary and slides its way down the tube to the uterus. While the egg travels, the walls of the uterus are becoming thick with blood and tissue to act as "bumper pads" for the egg. Once the egg reaches the uterus, it waits to be fertilized by a sperm. If the egg gets fertilized by a sperm, the egg plants itself in the blood "bumper pads" lining and grows into a baby. When the egg doesn't get fertilized, the uterus decides to clean house and flush all the extra blood "padding" it made and push the egg through your vagina. This is your period.

The Merry-Go-Round Cycle

The average menstrual cycle last 28 days, but can vary from girl to girl. A period generally lasts 5 to 7 days. The lining or padding of the uterus then begins to build up again about 2 weeks after the last period. The process starts again when the ovaries release another egg.

While some periods may last only a few days, others will last a week. Some girls may experience very heavy bleeding in the first couple of days, while others have a light period for a week. You may feel like you are losing a lot of blood during your period, but it is actually only a few spoonfuls to a cup of blood. **EVERY GIRL IS DIFFERENT.** It will take your body about a year or so to become regular. In the beginning, you may have one period then skip the next month. This is normal, too. If you are concerned about your period lasting several weeks or if you go six months without having a period after starting your menstrual cycle, you should contact a doctor. If you have other questions or concerns about what's going on inside your body, talk to your mom or another female adult you can trust. They will understand because they have been through it too.

The Ups and Downs of PMS

You may experience some of these symptoms while menstruating:

- ✳ cramps
- ✳ mood swings
- ✳ bloating
- ✳ tender breasts
- ✳ headache
- ✳ fatigue
- ✳ irritability

For some girls they can be mild, while for others these symptoms can be severe both physically and emotionally. This is called premenstrual syndrome (PMS). In other words, you suddenly feel like a pit bull with lipstick on! This is quite common for women and any girl can experience some of these symptoms before their period starts. The good news is the symptoms usually subside after your period starts. The causes for PMS are unknown, but many believe it is related to a woman's change in hormones or a vitamin deficiency.

✳ ✳✳ ✳ ✳✳ ✳ ✳✳ ✳ ✳✳ ✳ ✳✳

Head-To-Toe Tip

Ways to Ease PMS

There a several things you can do to ease the symptoms of PMS. Here's just a few:

❋ exercise regularly

❋ avoid caffeine and sweets

❋ rest with a heating pad on your lower abdomen

Your First Period

Even though you won't know exactly when you will get your first period, you can be prepared by having a supply of pads and panty liners on hand. You may want to carry one in your purse, so if you are at school or at the mall, it won't take you by surprise.

There are several different feminine hygiene products from which to choose.

PADS

Pads fit into your underwear with a sticky strip on the back to hold them in place. They come in various sizes and thickness, depending on your menstrual flow. You will need to change your pad every 3 to 4 hours, depending on how heavy your flow is.

LINERS

Panty liners are very thin pads and are great for days when you are light or are near the end of your period. Once you notice your flow is starting to slow down and is almost finished, you will want to use a liner for a day or so afterwards for extra protection.

TAMPONS

Tampons are good for active girls who can't let a period get in the way of their activities like swimming or ballet dancing. You will want to discuss using these with your mom before trying it alone.

Keep Track

You will want to keep track of when you start your period on a calendar to see how long it lasts and when you can expect the next one. After a year or so, your cycle will become more regular and you'll be able to figure it on your own.

Set Apart Time

The Bible says a woman is "unclean" for seven days during her menstruation and is set-apart for the Lord during this time. In Ancient times, a woman would sit in her tent alone while family members waited on her, treating her like royalty. On the eighth day she would immerse herself in a pool of moving, "living water" called a Mikveh (Hebrew word for baptism) as an act of spiritual purification and rebirth to become "clean." This practice is quite similar to what Christian believers do today in baptism as a sign of repentance and becoming "born again." As a believer in Jesus, you too have been made "clean" through the blood of Jesus that He shed on the cross. As a believer, you are now set apart as His alone.

InstaMssg Irene:
Teased

Dear Irene:

A guy in my class said to me, "You must be on the rag" because I was upset about something. What was he talking about?

Teased

Dear Teased:

That is just a crude nickname for your period. In olden times, women didn't have disposable pads like we do today and had to use "rags" while they were on their period. You will probably hear other terms like, "time of the month," "little friend," "the curse," and "joining the red jello club," etc. Boys will be boys, at least until they grow up anyway. So try not to let it bother you. It's all natural and part of being a woman!

Irene

Make IT! Candy Apple Shower Gel

Relive all of your fond memories of picking apples in the fall when you use this delicious shower treat. Shower time hasn't ever been this tasty.

What You Will Need:

※ decorative bottle or plastic container with lid

※ mixing bowl

※ 5 drops apple fragrance oil

※ 5 drops red food coloring

※ 4 cups distilled water

※ 1 cup unscented shampoo (mild baby shampoo can also be used as a substitute)

※ 1 ½ ounces liquid glycerin* (acts as a skin moisturizer)

What To Do:

1. In a mixing bowl, add all ingredients and stir well.

2. Pour shower gel into a bottle or plastic container for storage until use.

3. Use as you would soap in shower or add to running water for a bubble bath.

*liquid glycerin can be purchased at any health food store, craft store, and some drug stores.

There is a time for everything, and a season for every activity under heaven.
Ecclesiastes 3:1

Try This:

Is there anything you feel **ANXiOUS** about today?

Draw a picture of you giving your problem or care to God.

Chapter Six

Dare to Dream Beauty Rest

Find rest, O my soul, in God alone;
my hope comes from him.
~Psalm 62:5

Every girl needs rest to be healthy. **MOST GIRLS NEED AT LEAST EIGHT HOURS OF SLEEP**, but during this time of change for you, you may find you need 10 hours or more. That's okay, too. Once you figure out how much rest your body requires, stick with the same amount every night, even if it's summer time and there's no school, so you'll wake up refreshed and ready to face the day.

There are times though, when the sandman doesn't come to bring you a dream and you can't fall asleep. If this is the case, try these tips so you can get a great night's sleep.

Head-To-Toe Tip

Counting Sheep to a Great Night's Sleep

✻ Avoid drinking sodas with caffeine, a chemical that keeps you awake and makes you feel edgy at night.

✻ No Sleeping In. Even if you had a poor night's sleep, get up at your normal time. This will ensure a better night's sleep for the next night.

✳ Get up at the same time every day. If you start going to bed later and sleeping in the next morning, after a few days your body clock will reset itself to match your new schedule. Suddenly, you will find yourself lying in bed awake unable to go to sleep and oversleeping in the morning.

✳ Set your body's alarm clock. By opening the window blinds or stepping outside to get some sunshine in the morning, your body knows it is daytime and time to get up.

✳ Do physical activity during the day, especially on days after a bad night's sleep. Aerobic activity during the afternoon will promote more restful sleep. Stretching before bed is another way to get a good night's sleep.

✳ Hide your digital clock, especially if it lights up the room. You might be tempted to stare at it and be anxious about how much time has passed since you went to bed.

✳ Don't take a nap. Even though you may feel like you need one after having a rough night wrestling with the bedcovers, stay busy.

✳ Set a bedtime. As awful as it sounds, having a set time every night will help your body get into a healthy routine. Your body will expect it.

✳ Start a bedtime routine. Stop studying and doing homework a half-hour before bed. Do something relaxing like reading your Bible, listening to soothing music, or writing in your journal. These kinds of activities will soothe your mind into la-la land.

 ✳ Take a warm bath before bed. This will help relax your muscles. Avoid showers since these are stimulating.

✳ Wear socks to bed. Feet tend to feel colder at night, due to poor circulation. Studies show that keeping your footsies warm will reduce night wakings.

✳ No TV right before bed. It's a good idea to not have one in the bedroom either. It stimulates your brain and makes it difficult to fall to sleep.

✳ Keep a pad and pencil by the bed for jotting "to-do's." That way you won't spend the whole night staying awake trying to remember something you left out of the book report you did.

✳ Don't eat a heavy meal before bed. Eat dinner at least four hours before bed to ensure it is completely digested.

✳ Warm milk does your sleep good. A glass at bedtime stimulates the brain to produce serotonin, which helps you sleep.

✳ Use white noise. If you live in noisy surroundings, sometimes it helps to have a fan running to drown out other noises that make it difficult to sleep. And, there are always ear plugs, if necessary.

✳ Waking up after a few hours sleep? Don't get up and eat or drink anything. Your body will start to wake for special treats every night. Do get up out of bed and read a little or write in your journal or do another quiet activity.

✳ Don't make yourself sleep. If after a half-hour or so of lying in bed awake, get up out of your bed and sit in a chair to read or listen to a relaxing CD.

Keep a Sleep Diary

You can learn more about your sleep pattern by keeping a daily sleep diary. Include your dreams if you can remember them and see what's playing in the theater of your mind.

Sleep Diary

Bedtime: _____ Time Woke Up: _____

Total Sleep Hours: _____ Quality of Sleep: _____

Times You Were Awake, if any:

_____

What Did You Do During Wake Times:

_____

_____

Food Before Bed:

_____

Other Things I Did Before Bed:

_____

DreamNotes: _____

_____

_____

What It Was About:

_____

_____

_____

InstaMssg Irene:
Can't Sleep

Dear Irene:

Sometimes I can't sleep at night because I worry about not passing a test or I can't stop thinking about a project that's almost due. I have tried counting sheep and everything and nothing seems to work. I just lie in bed staring at the ceiling waiting for morning. I'm exhausted by morning when the alarm goes off. What should I do?

Can't Sleep

Dear Can't Sleep:

Not being able to sleep at night is called insomnia and everyone experiences it now and then. There are several things you will want to try for getting a good night's rest. For instance, after 20-30 minutes, get out of bed and try reading in a chair for a while. This will take your mind off the textbooks and help you unwind. Listening to soft, relaxing music while you doze off may help, too. But, whatever you do, don't fight it. Worrying about a test or project at night will only make matters worse for you. Just know the next night you will be good and tired and ready for bed. Most importantly, if school work has got you upset, you will want to talk to your parents or school teacher about that. They can help you develop better study habits so you will be prepared for your tests and help you complete your projects. In no time, you'll be getting the zzzzzz's you need and ready to go in the morning.

Irene

InstaMssg Irene:
Nightmare on Ellie's Street

Dear Irene:

I had this dream that my family moved into a wonderful old
Victorian-style house with a large porch. As I am walking to the back
of the house I go into my room. Outside of my window are lots of
trees and it's really dark. Suddenly, someone climbs into my room
through the window and grabs me. That's when I wake up. I'm
scared.

Nightmare Ellie

Dear Nightmare Ellie:

Stressful thoughts like worrying about the boogie man getting you
can turn sweet dreams into nightmares. When you sleep, your brain
doesn't turn off. It goes through several sleep stages, including
REM, which is Rapid Eye Movement. During this stage, your eyes
move back and forth under your closed eyelids. This is when you
are dreaming and sometimes they can be good, other times the
dreams are bad. Many times girls will have nightmares because they
are dealing with problems at school or because of a major change
like moving into a new house. Other reasons for having nightmares
may be from watching scary movies before bed or when you are
sick and have a high fever (medication sometimes causes girls to
have strange "pink elephant" dreams). Let your parents know if this
happens especially if you are taking medicine. The good news about
nightmares is they aren't real and can't hurt you. Don't forget to
pray before you go to sleep at night.

Irene

Fill-in blanks to complete this scripture:

"I will _____ down and _____ in _____, for you alone, O LORD, make _____ dwell in _____.

Psalm 4:8

Make IT! Sleepy-Time Tea

When zzzzzzzzzzz's are lacking and you just can't seem to get to sleep, here is a tea that will quiet your mind and soothe away all your worries.

What You Will Need:

- ✳ saucepan
- ✳ 1 fresh coffee filter
- ✳ ¼ teaspoon powdered ginger
- ✳ ¼ teaspoon powdered cinnamon
- ✳ ¼ teaspoon catnip or fresh mint (catnip can purchased at any health food store and some fresh produce grocers)
- ✳ 2 teaspoons sugar

What To Do:

1. Heat hot water in a saucepan. Or, you can use hot tap water from your kitchen sink.

2. Spoon all ingredients into a coffee filter and twist together. Let it seep in your cup of hot water for a few minutes.

3. Add sugar for taste. For variations, try adding honey or milk. Enjoy!

Make IT! Cotton Candy Bubble Bath

Soothe away all your troubles in this relaxing and fragrant treat. It's simple and easy to make. You can also make it for gifts for friends and loved ones for any special occasion. It works well as a body wash, too.

What You Will Need:

- ❋ mixing bowl
- ❋ decorative bottle or plastic container with lid
- ❋ ½ cup unscented shampoo (or you can use mild baby shampoo as a substitute)
- ❋ ¾ cup water
- ❋ ½ teaspoon table salt
- ❋ 15 drops cherry fragrance oil (or you can substitute with your favorite essential oil)

What To Do:

1. Pour shampoo into the mixing bowl. Add water.
2. Stir mixture until well blended. Add salt and stir until liquid thickens.
3. Add cherry fragrance and stir.
4. Pour bubble bath into a decorative bottle or plastic container. Enjoy!

How Can You Sleep At a Time Like This?

Does the sound of rain pounding your window pane keep you awake or help you sleep? How about when thunder crashes loudly nearby and lightning flashing across the night sky? Most people wake up during a big storm — but not Jesus.

Matthew 8:23-27 tells about a time when Jesus and his disciples were on a boat and a furious storm came up without warning. While the waves swept over the boat, Jesus stayed fast asleep. The disciples probably wondered how Jesus could sleep at a time like this, so they woke him and said, "Lord, save us! We're going to drown!" Even though they were terrified, He wasn't. Jesus rebuked the winds and the waves and everything suddenly became calm. Naturally, this amazed the disciples, but Jesus replied, "You of little faith, why are you so afraid?" In other words Jesus was assuring the disciples that He had everything under control.

Bed Check

Tonight I Feel:

☑ Sleepy	☐ Exhausted	☐ Wide awake
☑ Peaceful	☐ Groggy	☐ Perky
☐ Dozy	☐ Restless	☐ Bustling
☐ Drowsy	☐ Alert	☐ Totally wired
☑ Tired	☐ Excited	

Come to me, all you who are weary and burdened, and I will give you rest. Take my yoke upon you and learn from me, for I am gentle and humble in heart, and you will find rest for your souls.

Matthew 11:28-29

Celebrating with God Devotion:
Pots of Gold

"Wait a minute, guys. I am still trying to get this mop to stay in place," Marisa complained while fixing her hair.

"Would you stop primping so much in the mirror? Your hair looks fine," Alexis responded, trying to get her friend to leave the school bathroom.

"Marisa, we have to meet my parents in the cafeteria in two minutes!" Suzie tugged at her friend's blue jacket. "Our projects are going be judged soon. Let's go!"

The three girls quickly made their way through the crowd of students and parents waiting near the entrance of the art department at Hermitage Middle. Colorful banners dangled from the ceiling, and art projects lined the hallway. Speakers boomed overhead, announcing the sections to be judged next. Suzie wiped her frizzy red hair out of her eyes and scanned the room for her parents. Finally spotting them near the pottery display, she waved and ran over with Marisa and Alexis close behind.

"Hi, girls, I'm glad to see you made it in time." Mrs. Park smiled, looking at her watch.

"I was looking for your pots, but I can't find them among all these wonderful projects." Mr. Park gazed down the row. "Can you girls show me yours?"

Suzie and Marisa excitedly led the way to their pots. Marisa snatched hers up and proudly showed it to the group.

"I used lots of gold glitter and gems for mine and the colors are the same colors as the Jamaican flag, where my family is from." Marisa beamed, her black braids bouncing. "This contest will be a cinch," she continued with her deep brown eyes sparkling.

Suzie carefully picked her pot up. "I didn't use very many bright colors or sparkles, but I worked really hard on it."

After the judges closely examined each piece of pottery for soundness, quality, and beauty, the girls dashed to their projects. Suzie worried for a moment, but then felt relief when she saw a flutter of blue.

"My pot won first place!" she squealed with delight.

"Great job, Suzie!" Alexis gave her friend a high-five. "How did you do, Marisa?"

Marisa fingered the red second place ribbon hanging on her pot. "I didn't win first place." She said looking down.

Alexis looked at Marisa's pot. "Your pot is certainly beautiful on the outside, but look inside." She showed Marisa the cracked interior.

"Isn't that sort of like something in the Bible?" Suzie asked.

Alexis thought for a moment. "Yeah, it's like how God looks at our hearts. He's not as concerned about our outward appearance as much as our heart and relationship with Him."

Marisa smiled. "Maybe my pot didn't win, but with God as my judge, my heart wins first place with Him."

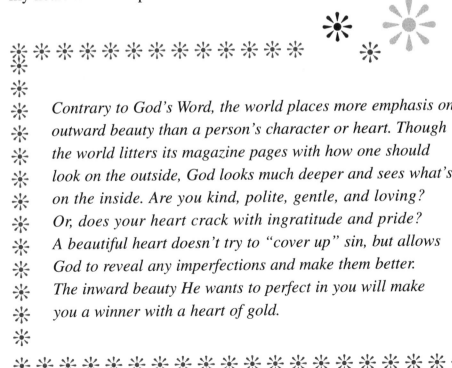

Contrary to God's Word, the world places more emphasis on outward beauty than a person's character or heart. Though the world litters its magazine pages with how one should look on the outside, God looks much deeper and sees what's on the inside. Are you kind, polite, gentle, and loving? Or, does your heart crack with ingratitude and pride? A beautiful heart doesn't try to "cover up" sin, but allows God to reveal any imperfections and make them better. The inward beauty He wants to perfect in you will make you a winner with a heart of gold.

Try This:

Write a prayer to God asking Him to help you when you feel **FRUSTRATED** or can't sleep at night.

Chapter Seven

The Finish Line on Fitness

Everyone who competes in the games
goes into strict training. They do it to get a crown
that will not last; but we do it to get a crown
that will last forever.

~1 Corinthians 9:25

On Your Marks, Get Set, GO!

Vibrant girls like you know that looking good on the outside is about feeling good on the inside. Regular exercise plays an important role in how we look and feel.

Exercise will

> *make your heart and muscles strong,*
>> *give you energy to tackle the day,*
>>> *give you better and more restful sleep,*
>>>> *burn fat and tone your body,*
>>>>> *and give you confidence.*

Do you know of anything else that can do all that? So, get moving and learn how to get fit, practice sports safety, and **HAVE FUN!**

How Fit are You?

Fitness isn't just about Stairmasters and lifting weights, it's about benefitting you for everyday life. Are you able to climb the stairs without losing your breath? Can you carry a full trash can around the house without huffing and puffing? Take this quick quiz to find out.

1. HOW FLEXIBLE are YOU? Stand and cross your legs. Bend at the waist with your arms dangling in front of you: don't bounce or bend your knees. Try to touch the floor in front of your toes with your fingers.

A. Does touching my knees count?
   You can't reach anywhere close to your feet.

B. You can touch your feet, well almost.

C. No problem. You can touch the floor.

2. DO YOU HAVE ENERGY TO SPARE? Try running up a flight of stairs without stopping until you reach the top.

A. You feel too winded to answer this quiz.

B. You are breathing faster than usual, but can talk to others.

C. Piece of cake. You're ready to hit the next flight of stairs.

3. HOW HARDY ARE YOU? Walk a mile, as fast as you can. Record how long it takes you.

A. See you next week. It takes you more than 20 minutes (okay, forever) to walk the mile.

B. As long as there is a good reason, you finish the mile in 15-20 minutes.

C. Wow, that was easy. You finished in less than 15 minutes.

4. HOW STRONG ARE YOU? Try doing push-ups continuously. (Hand on the floor, just under your shoulders with knees and toes touching the ground.)

A. You finished five push-ups in a row and that was a struggle.

B. Not so bad after all. You finished ten push-ups in a row.

C. Like taking candy from a baby. You finished fifteen push-ups in a row.

5. HOW ACTIVE ARE YOU? How many minutes a day do you get your heart rate up? Think about all the activities you do during the day like gym class, tennis practice, etc.

A. Does making popcorn count? You are active for less than 20 minutes a day.

B. You are active for 45 minutes to an hour a day, easy.

C. Every minute counts in your busy schedule. You can't even list all the activities you do. You are definitely active for more than an hour a day.

IF YOU ANSWERED MOSTLY A'S: Honey, its time we talked. You need to get some motion in the loco-motion. If you are a beginner at this (in other words, it's been a while since you really made any kind of effort to get fit), be sure and take it slow and easy with stretching to start. Only do as much as you can without strain or pain. Try to make a commitment to do some form of exercise every day to get you back in shape.

IF YOU ANSWERED MOSTLY B'S: Girlfriend, you are fit but could work on improving some of the areas where you scored the lowest. Try adding stretches to your schedule, walk more, and add hand weights (see Homemade Hand Weights on page 118) to your workout program to build upper body strength.

IF YOU ANSWERED MOSTLY C'S: Girl, you are fit. Good for you! You know an active girl is a healthy girl. Keep up the good work and be sure to stay flexible by stretching for 10 minutes every-day. Add variety to your exercise routine with new stretches and work on weak spots that need your attention.

Good Vibrations Heartbeat Activity

Here's a way to actually see your heartbeat.

What You Need:

✳ a bath scale (a manual scale with a spinning dial, not a digital one)

What To Do:

1. Run around the house and do some cartwheels, jumping jacks, etc., to get your heart beating fast.

2. Stand on the scale and watch the needle move.

You should be able to see it move in time with your heart rate. Your body is racing to circulate the blood in your body, carrying oxygen to all the muscles that are burning fuel. Your heart has to work extra hard when you exercise and in this case you are seeing the "good vibrations."

Dos and Dont's of Exercise

Before starting any kind of exercise or sports program, it's good to know the "dos" and "don'ts" that will keep you in the game.

Do Wear the Right Gear

Your parents have probably already told you a hundred times not to forget to wear your helmet when rollerblading or bicycling. Also, don't forget the wrist and elbow pads and knee guards to protect those, too.

Don't Go Overboard

When you are just starting out in any sport or exercise program, listen to your body. It is telling to you something important if you begin to feel dizzy or sick to your stomach; can't catch your breath or are in pain. Sit down and rest and let your coach or parent know when this is happening.

Do Drink Lots of Water

Your body needs lots of fluid, so keep a sports bottle handy. A girl's sweat glands are hard at work releasing sweat to keep your skin cool during a workout. So, be sure to drink lots of water before, during, and after you exercise.

Don't Forget to Warm Up

Be sure to do warm-ups three to five minutes before stretching. The warm up will increase elasticity of the muscles and help prevent injury.

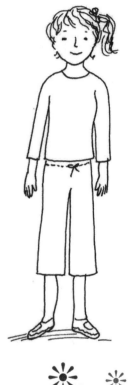

Do Wear Comfortable Clothing

It is not necessary to wear heavy sweats or a silver spacesuit to lose those unwanted pounds. You won't lose any more weight, you'll just sweat a lot more. Choose something that is loose fitting and comfortable. Some girls like to wear a special outfit that will put them in the mood for fitness.

Don't Forget to Cool Down

At the end of your workout, you will want to finish by slowing down your body with gentle stretching. This will help lower your body temperature and prevent stiffness in the morning.

Do Get Into a Routine

Experts agree girls need to stay on-the-go with some form of aerobic exercise three times a week, with each workout lasting at least 20 minutes. Aerobic exercise is anything that gets your heart rate up and speeds up your breathing.

Your Workout

In order to build and improve muscle strength, it is important to have an aerobic program (exercise that requires oxygen and gets your heart pumping) as part of your weekly routine. This will ensure you have more energy, look better, and feel stronger as you get more physically fit. **OKay, SO WHaT aRe yOU WaiTiNG FOR?** Put down the remote and give the television a rest. Its time to work out, girlfriend!

Your workout doesn't have to be boring or a chore to do. Find unique and creative ways to add fun to your fitness schedule. Choose activities you will enjoy, so you will stick with your exercise program. Of course you are going to want to do something that will excite you and make you want to do it again.

The activity you choose should fit your style and not make you feel uncomfortable or klutzy. If you aren't good at dribbling a ball and can't shoot worth a hoot, why bother taking up basketball as your exercise program? It is a good idea to try something new and experiment, but if it isn't your cup of tea, try something different.

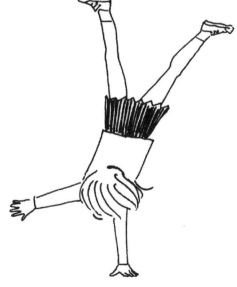

Even though surfing sounds adventurous, how practical is it for you? Will you be able to get to the beach every week to practice? Do you own a board? Try choosing an activity that will not require a lot of effort and expense, like jogging, or bicycling. The easier for you to do your workout, the less likely you will skip your scheduled workout.

If you do choose to take karate classes or something that requires money, make sure it is something that fits within your budget. Be sure to discuss this with your parents and make sure it is something they want you to commit to.

Find a sport or activity that suits you. If you thrive on being with other people, then team sports might be a nice fit. However, if you prefer doing it alone, swimming at the YMCA or running at the school track may suit you better. Choose an activity that matches your personality and interests.

Consider how much time you have for your work-out schedule. There are no set rules for how much time you need to do exercise. However, if you only have a couple of hours each week to devote to exercise, it may work better for you to find something nearby or on the way home from school. Better yet, how about volunteering at home for aerobic chores like raking leaves or sweeping the patio?

If you find yourself falling into an exercise rut and can't seem to come up with anything interesting, stay flexible by working on your stretches in Twist and Shout Stretches on page 119. These can be done anywhere: at home, at school while standing in the lunch line, or at the bus stop.

Setting Goals

When it comes to exercising, one of the most important things you can do is set goals to keep track of your progress so you can see how far you have come. Do you know what you want to accomplish with this exercise program? Try making a list of all the goals you want to accomplish. For instance, you might want to try out for the cheerleading squad, but you have never done any of the jumps before. You will need to break down your goal into smaller, more manageable pieces (like learning how to do a cartwheel). This will keep you from failing to reach your final goal and giving up. To accomplish this, you will need to work on certain muscle groups to strengthen your arms and upper body and of course, practice, practice, practice. Most people are surprised at the weekly effort it takes to reach their goals. But, you can have success if your goal isn't impossible to reach.

Naturally, the hardest part will be sticking to your routine. That is why you will want to schedule your exercise sessions each week and write them down in your fitness journal (you can make one using a blank notebook) or use the following *Fitness Journal* form. Set weekly goals and be sure to reward yourself with a treat when you reach your goal. Celebrate your successes; you deserve it. The more you accomplish, the better will feel about yourself. Then, you can start setting bigger goals for yourself as time goes on.

Fitness Journal: Goal Setter

Name: _____ Date: _____

My Ultimate Goal:

_____

_____

_____

Ultimate Target Date: _____ (it will be reached)

Action I Must Take To Reach Ultimate Goal:

Step #1:

_____

_____

Date Step #1 will be reached: _____

Step #2:

_____

_____

Date Step #2 will be reached: _____

Step #3:

_____

_____

Date Step #3 will be reached: _____

Other Steps:

_____

_____

Date Other Steps will be reached: _____

_____

_____

_____

How I will stay on track with steps:

_____

POTENTIAL PROBLEMS:

_____

_____

How To Resolve Problem:

_____

_____

Fitness Journal: Workout Log Week of: _____

Name: _____Hours of Sleep: _____

Glasses of Water: 1 2 3 4 5 6 7 8

Vitamin: _____ Calcium: _____

EXERCISE:

Aerobic _____ Duration: _____

Date: _____

_____

_____

_____

_____

_____

Stretches: _____ Duration: _____

Date: _____

_____

_____

_____

_____

FOOD/DIET NOTES:

_____

_____

_____

_____

_____

_____

_____

InstaMssg Irene:
Thigh Busters

Dear Irene:

Last weekend I got to stay up late and watch TV. An infomercial came on talking about this wonderful new thighbuster. I begged my mom to let me get it. She said, "No way!" I really need it, because I hate the way my thighs look.

Tyra

Dear Tyra:

Infomercials promise everything from dazzling clean clothes to amazingly thin thighs in just minutes a day. While this sounds really good at 2 am, don't let your fuzzy, sleep-deprived brain trick you into one of these crazy schemes. Your mom is right. There is no miracle cure or magic potion or incredible machine that can replace good ol' exercise along with a healthy diet and proper rest. It's up to you, girlfriend.

Irene

InstaMssg Irene:
The Sloucher

Dear Irene:

My mom is always telling me to "stop slouching" when I am doing my homework. I don't even realize that I am doing it. I just want to be comfortable. Help!

The Sloucher

Dear Sloucher:

Good health begins with good posture, they say. One of the main reasons people slouch is due to fatigue, and then a snowball effect of other health concerns kick in like shallow breathing and back problems, not to mention poor eyesight because of improper posture. It's a fine balancing act between being comfortable and just being plain lazy. Whether sitting or standing, you need to strengthen your back and abdominal muscles by holding yourself upright. Exercise will help you get your back in shape.

Try this at home: the next time you are studying and need a break, take your textbook and place it on your head while sitting. Once you feel the book is balanced on your head, slowly stand up and walk around the room. When you get pretty good at it, try hopping on one foot with the book on your head. Ok, hit those books and get studying again.

Irene

 **Handmade Hand Weights**

You won't need to purchase expensive equipment. Barbells have never been closer — in the kitchen! These will help build up your biceps.

What To Do:

1. Grab two cans of vegetables (16-ounce) to use as weights. For smaller hands, use smaller cans.
2. Holding one can in each hand, stand with your feet shoulder-width apart.
3. With your arms extended straight and your palms facing down toward your body, lift the weights while keeping your arms straight until they reach shoulder level.
4. Slowly lower your arms to your legs; repeat this exercise 10 times.

First Things First

Before you start any exercise program, it is important to check first with your parents and family physician to make sure that you don't have any health conditions that should be taken into consideration.

Twist and Shout Stretches

Twist and Shout stretches are exercises you can include in both your warm-up and cool-down routine. When done properly, these stretches during your warm-up will help you become more flexible, reducing your chance of suffering injury during a game and helping you perform more skillfully. When included in your cool-down session, these exercises will help reduce muscular soreness and tension later, not to mention help you relax and sleep better. And finally, one of the best benefits is they help reduce the severity of painful menstruation, which every girl can live without.

Get Stretched

When starting a stretch exercise, try to focus on the muscles being stretched and push yourself to test the outer limit of movement. Avoid bouncing, as this can cause muscular tissue damage and will only create unnecessary pain. Breathe normally during each stretch and try to not hold your breath. Once you're extended, hold that position for 20 seconds. Choose 6–9 stretches and try doing them 6 times a week (take the Sabbath off and give your body a rest). You should be finished in about 3 minutes. In a few weeks you will feel a noticeable difference and be more limber. After 2–3 months, try adding new stretches to your routine that will increase your flexibility and enhance your fitness goals. Before you know it, you will be flying through the air for the volleyball in gym class like Wonder Woman.

Terrific Towel Stretches

No fancy equipment required.
These exercises only require a hand towel.

What To Do:

1. While standing, grip the towel with both hands slightly wider than shoulder-width apart.

2. Slowly lift the towel over your head with arms extended and down behind your back. (Towel should be parallel with the floor)

3. Repeat this exercise 10 times. For greater flexibility, try moving hands closer together and repeat exercise.

Towel Stretch #2

1. While standing, hold one end of the towel with your left hand and bend your elbow behind your head to drape towel over your back lengthwise. (Towel should be parallel with your body.)

2. Grab the other end of the towel with your right hand.

3. Slowly straighten your left hand over your head continuing to hold onto the towel. You should feel your muscles stretch in your arms.

4. Hold this position for 10 seconds. To prevent arching your back, tighten your abdominal muscles.

5. Slowly bend your left elbow and lower towel down your back, straightening your right arm.

6. Hold this position for 10 seconds. Switch sides and repeat this exercise 10 times.

Towel Stretch #3

1. While standing, hold each end of the towel with both hands shoulder-width apart. Knees should be slightly bent.

2. Lift arms with towel outstretched to shoulder level. Slowly lift over your head. (Towel should be parallel with the floor.)

3. Slowly bend to one side, without twisting. Hold this position for 10 seconds.

4. Return to standing position, then bend to the other side. Hold this position for 10 seconds.

5. Repeat this exercise 10 times for each side.

Hop Socks

This exercise tests your balance and lets you know if you would be good at a sport that requires this skill such as a windsurfing or snow skiing.

What To Do:

1. Standing on a tile or bare wood floor while wearing only socks, place your foot against the knee of your dominant leg (the one you use to kick a ball) and place your hands on your hips.

2. Ask a friend with a secondhand watch to help you. When 5 seconds have gone by, make a half turn on the ball of your foot.

3. Keep turning every 5 seconds until you lose your balance and take your foot off of your knee or your hands off of your hips.

Posture Press & Pulls

Presses are a great exercise to try during your cool down. It is also good for helping you relax before bed. Pulls will strengthen your abs (abdominal) and back muscles, helping you keep a good posture.

What To Do For Presses:

1. Lie face down on your bed flat on your stomach. (You may use a pillow under your stomach for support if you like.)

2. In a push-up position with elbows bent at shoulder level, slowly lift your upper body (head, shoulders, and chest) off the bed, keeping your hips and lower body flat on the bed.

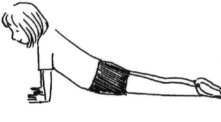

3. Hold this position for 10 seconds (You should not be feeling any strain or pain in your lower back if done correctly.)

4. Lower your body down to the bed and repeat 5-10 times.

What To Do For Pulls:

1. Lie face down on your bed. (You may use a pillow under your head if you like.)

2. In a push-up position with elbows bent at shoulder level, slowly lift your body (head, shoulders, chest, stomach, hips) off the bed,

keeping your legs straight, bending at the knees (knees should be touching the bed).

3. Curl body into a sitting position, sitting on your lower legs and heels.

4. Lower your body down into the flat position and repeat 5-10 times.

Back Scratch Stretch

This stretch is great for your cool down routine after a rigorous workout.

What To Do:

1. Lying on your back, stretch arms and legs straight out. Stretch arms over your head and legs spread apart.

2. Reach as far as you can in all directions. Hold this position for 10 seconds. Don't forget to breathe.

3. Now, wiggle your back from side to side and relax.

4. Let all your muscles go limp for a few seconds, then repeat this stretch several more times.

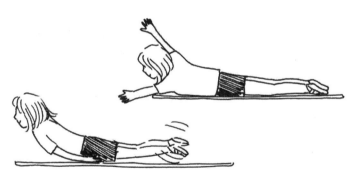

Footsie's Twist

If you are a dancer, this great stretch will keep you on your toes.

What To Do:

1. Sit on the floor with your legs straight and toes pointed away from your body.

2. Flex your ankles with your toes pointing up toward the ceiling.

3. Rotate your feet together, making big circles with your toes.

4. Squeeze your toes together tightly, making two clockwise circles. Now, make two circles going counterclockwise.

5. Spread your toes apart and stretch. Repeat this exercise 8-10 times.

Twisters

This stretch is designed to help strengthen your muscles in your lower back and hips. It help prepares you for activities such as swinging the bat at the softball game or the triple-twist jump in ice-skating.

What To Do:

1. Lie down on your back with your knees bent and your feet flat on the floor.

2. Pull feet close to your buttocks and stretch your arms straight out at your sides at shoulder level.

3. Slowly rotate your knees to one side, then the other. Be sure to keep knees together.

4. Lift both arms off the floor at the same time with palms facing each other. Slowly bring together, keeping them straight, then back down to the floor. Repeat steps three and four 10 times.

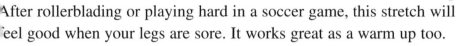

Leg Counts

After rollerblading or playing hard in a soccer game, this stretch will feel good when your legs are sore. It works great as a warm up too.

What To Do:

1. Lying flat on your back, wrap both arms around your bent knees and pull into your chest.

2. While knees still bent, grab your feet with both hands.

3. Slowly straighten your legs (as much as you can without causing pain) still holding onto your feet. Flex feet with toes pulled down and heels pointing toward ceiling.

4. Hold this position for 10 seconds.

5. Bend your knees and wrap your arms around your legs to bring into your chest.

6. Repeat complete exercise 10 times.

Arm Circles

A young lady knows how important it is to keep her shoulders back and work on her posture. This exercise will strengthen muscles in your upper body and shoulders.

What To Do:

1. Stand with feet shoulder-width apart and toes facing forward. Hold your arms straight out at shoulder level and palms facing up.

2. Tighten your abdominal muscles and buttocks and bend knees slightly.

3. With your shoulders, arms, and hands make circular motions.

4. Repeat this exercise 10 times, alternating palms facing toward the ceiling and down toward the floor.

5. Once you have mastered this exercise, try using your Homemade Hand Weights while making circular motions.

Bed Sits

This exercise will help flatten the tummy and strengthen your abs.

What To Do:

1. Lie on the floor with your legs up and over the bed. Your buttocks will be pressing against the edge of your bed. If you bed is too high for your legs to reach, try using a couch or chair for this exercise.

2. With your chin tucked and arms folded across your chest, lift your head, shoulders, and chest off the floor in a sitting up position. Be sure to keep legs resting on the bed.

3. Exhale when you lift off the floor and inhale when you return to your starting position.

4. Repeat 10 times (try adding one each day as you progress).

Leg Lifts

For the dancer or karate champion in you, this exercise will strengthen the outer thigh and hip muscles, providing more proficiency in your side-to-side moves.

What To Do:

1. Lying on your side, extend your arm beneath your head.

2. With your other arm bent at the elbow, place your palm face down in front of your chest to stay balanced and keep from rolling.

3. Keeping your leg straight, lift as far as you can. Point your toes and facing forward.

4. Switch sides and repeat 5-10 times for each leg.

Curls

Here is an exercise you can do using your Homemade Hand Weights. This will strengthen your shoulders and upper muscles of your arms.

What To Do:

1. Standing with your feet shoulder-width apart, hold one hand weight in each hand with arms down by each side.

2. Slowly lift your arms with palms facing out, until straight out at shoulder level.

3. Lower your arms back down slowly to each side. Repeat 10 times.

4. Now, hold each hand weight with palms facing up toward the ceiling and slowly lift your arms straight until they reach shoulder level. Repeat 10 times.

5. Finally, hold each hand weight with palms facing up toward the ceiling and slowly bend your elbows and curl your hand weights up to your chest. Slowly bring weights down keeping your arms straight and repeat 10 times.

Fly Through the Air Workout

Here's a stretch that will send you soaring into perfect fitness. These stretches use almost all of your muscle groups.

What To Do:

1. Lie on the stomach face down with your arms down by your sides.

2. Lift your head and upper body off the floor. Legs and lower body should be resting on the floor. Stretch your arms out at your sides like wings.

3. Hold this position for as long as possible. Repeat 10 times.

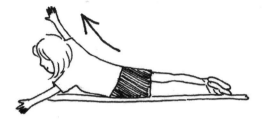

Workout #2:

1. Lie on the stomach face down with your arms down by your sides.
2. Without moving your arms, lift your head and upper body off the floor. Legs and lower body should be resting on the floor.
3. Hold this position for as long as possible. Lie back down and rest. Repeat 10 times.

Workout #3:

1. Lie on your stomach face down with your arms outstretched over your head.
2. Lift your legs together and hold this position for several seconds.
3. Keep your hips on the floor and try rocking back and forth. Repeat 10 times.

Workout #4:

1. Lie on your stomach face down with your arms down by your sides.
2. Lift your head and upper body off the floor.
3. With legs straight, spread apart slightly and kick back and forth. Repeat 10 times.

Clock Kicks

If you take ballet, you may have done this one before. It will help improve your flexibility.

What To Do:

1. Stand beside a kitchen or dining table and place one hand on the tabletop for balance. Your body will be facing the 12 o'clock position.

2. Lift your leg that is furthest from the table toward the ceiling and parallel with the floor.

3. Point your toe and hold this position for 10 seconds.

4. Slowly lower your leg and rest for a moment.

5. Then, lifting the same leg again, slowly rotate it in counterclockwise to the 9 o'clock position. Stop and hold this position for 10 seconds. Return again to the 12 o'clock position.

6. Repeat this exercise again, only lifting your leg and swinging it back behind you to the 3 o'clock position. Stop and hold this position for 10 seconds. Return again to the 12 o'clock position. Don't forget to point your toes.

7. Now, turn your body and face the opposite direction to exercise with your other leg and repeat steps #2 through #6.

Prayer: Commitment

Father, Your Word tells me to commit my plans to you and if I trust in you, you will do it. Here are some of the fitness goals I hope to accomplish: _____, _____, and _____. I commit these to you and believe you will help me to be faithful to work each day toward reaching them. Thank you. In Jesus' name, Amen.

Show me your _____, O LORD, teach me your _____; _____ me in your _____ and _____ me, for you are God my Savior, and my _____ is in you all _____ long.   *Psalm 25:4*

Gold Medal Fitness Hints

❋ Find a friend or family to exercise with, or plan a special outing to the park to play soccer or softball with a group of your friends.

❋ Use the stairs at school and the mall whenever possible instead of taking the elevator or escalator.

❋ Drink plenty of water before, during, and after exercising.

❋ Instead of running to the fridge during TV commercials, use that time to do sit-ups or jog around the house.

❋ Ask your mom or dad to let you walk the dog everyday. If you don't have one, see if a neighbor will let you walk theirs. It's also a great way to make extra cash, too.

❋ Find new ways to get in shape by adding variety to the standard jumping jacks and jogging in place. Better yet, join your school's pep squad or another favorite sport.

❋ If you start an exercise program, set reachable goals. At the end of the week reward yourself.

 *Love the Lord your God with all your heart and with all your soul and with all your mind and with all your strength.* Mark 12:30

First Aid Station

Accidents do happen and when it comes to an injury such as a sprained ankle, twist, or bruise you can be prepared by knowing these simple steps known as R.I.C.E.

Rest = Stop once you feel pain or know you injured yourself.

Ice = Apply ice to the injury to help reduce swelling and pain.

Compression = Wrap the strain or wound with a bandage to protect it from further injury.

Elevation = If a limb such as a leg or arm has been injured, raise it up on a chair or pillow to help reduce swelling.

Of course, these are only the initial steps to giving first aid. In case of an emergency, call 9-1-1 and a parent or another adult who can help you with additional medical attention.

Head-To-Toe Tip

Workout Safety Pointers

❋ Start out slowly to avoid injury and muscle soreness from trying to do too much on the first day.

❋ Try a different activity every other week, varying your workouts.

❋ Push yourself gradually, trying to get out of your comfort zone once a week.

❋ Schedule your workouts every other day or at least three times a week, but not every day. Give your body time to recover from your new workout schedule.

❋ Do your exercise at the same time every day. This way you will have a better chance of sticking with it.

❋ Before you start any program, it is important to check with your family physician and/or parents to make sure you don't have any health conditions that should be taken into consideration.

❋ If you don't understand how to do a particular exercise, have an older person go over the steps with you.

❋ Try to always exercise in a safe place, preferably with a friend. Never go off alone in an isolated area. If you go to a park or school playground to work out, be sure to go when other people are around.

❋ You should be able to carry on a conversation while exercising. If you are out of breath and can't talk, you are probably working too hard. Slow down.

❋ If you ever feel dizzy, light-headed, or sick to your stomach, stop immediately. Rest, cool off, and grab the water bottle.

Celebrating with God Devotion: The Baker County Horse Show

Whack! Marisa swung the golf club, slamming the bright green golf ball toward the windmill. Boooonng! The ball struck one of the paddles and rolled back toward the tee-off point.

"Oh, that was pathetic, Marisa," Suzie teased.

"I did better than you," Marisa countered, laughing at the six strokes Suzie had taken on her turn. She handed the club to Alexis. "It's your turn, Michelle Wie."

Alexis chuckled as she gripped the handle with both hands and swung with all her might. Ding! Her ball made it through to the other side, making a hole-in-one.

"Wow, great job, Alexis!" Suzie cheered.

"The final hole, too! You get to choose a prize!" Marisa shouted.

Alexis picked her prize, an inflatable club, and bopped her friends on the head with it.

"This is a great place to come and knock a bucket of balls around. I'm not sure how much longer my Dad will be, so let's just take a look around." Alexis and her friends started walking down toward the green.

"Hey, what's going on over there at the county stadium?" one of the girls asked.

"It looks like a horse show or something. Let's go see," Suzie answered.

The girls hurried and grabbed seats near the middle of the grandstand.

"The judging of the Juvenile English Pleasure Horse Walk and Trot will begin momentarily," a speaker blared.

As the horses and riders began circling the ring to warm up, the girls pointed out their choices for prettiest horse and the ones the thought might win. One girl, riding a chestnut mare, looked very familiar to the three.

"Hey Marisa, see that girl with the pink helmet?" Suzie pointed. "Doesn't she look like that really quiet girl in our math class?"

"You mean Britney?" Marisa shaded her eyes.

Alexis peered at the young girl. "Yeah, she does."

During the show, the girls watched the horses and riders trot, run, and jump around the ring, and listened to the names being announced.

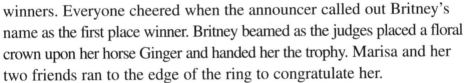

"Next we have Britney Moore and her horse, Ginger," the speaker blasted.

"It is her," the three friends exclaimed as they watched. Britney flawlessly trotted, ran, and jumped with her horse Ginger. After the last rider left the ring, the judges took a few minutes, then announced the winners. Everyone cheered when the announcer called out Britney's name as the first place winner. Britney beamed as the judges placed a floral crown upon her horse Ginger and handed her the trophy. Marisa and her two friends ran to the edge of the ring to congratulate her.

"Great job, Britney!" Suzie petted Ginger's nose.

"I didn't know you could ride so well," Alexis commented.

Marisa said, "Is this why we never see you at any of the club meetings or games after school?"

Britney smiled, "I would love to come to those, but I have to train everyday and take care of Ginger, my horse." She stroked Ginger's tan mane. "When I'm not riding, I am working at the stables to earn money for riding lessons and feed for Ginger."

"Wow, you really are dedicated!" Suzie smiled.

Alexis thought about what Britney said. "You know, that reminds me of what Paul said in the New Testament. He said we're supposed to train for the race, so we'll be qualified for the prize. And, if we persevere, we will win. Except, we won't win a crown like Ginger's. Will get a crown that will last forever!"

The Apostle Paul compared the Christian life to running a race because he knew athletes would understand that they have to train and get in shape before any competition. Believers too must train spiritually by studying the Scriptures and doing God's will in order to win the race God has placed them in. Like a marathon runner, you must continually keep your eyes on the prize, which is a crown in Heaven, so when you cross the finish line of life, you'll be a winner, too.

Pampered by The WORD

Everyone who competes in the games goes into strict training. They do it to get a crown that will not last; but we do it to get a crown that will last forever. Therefore I do not run like a man running aimlessly; I do not fight like a man beating the air. No, I beat my body and make it my slave so that after I have preached to others, I myself will not be disqualified for the prize.

1 Corinthians 9:25-27

Try This:

Sometimes we say or do silly things when we feel **Jealous.** Describe a time when you felt jealous.

What did you do?

Chapter Eight

Food for Thought on Healthly Eating

So whether you eat or drink or
whatever you do, do it all for the glory of God.
~1 Corinthians 10:31

Aren't hamburgers, nacho chips, and soda a balanced diet?

Not really. These are commonly referred to as "junk food," because they litter your body with junk like fat and offer little to no nutritional value. It's best to eat this kind of food sparingly, because a diet loaded down with junk food will make you feel sluggish and eventually make you sick. God doesn't want you to trash your temple with a poor diet, but wants you to feed your body the nutrients it needs to help you develop properly.

 **What to Eat and What Not to Eat**

The Bible literally has hundreds of Scriptures regarding what to eat, when to eat, what not to eat, and how to prepare it. Test your know-how by circling all the foods below that God gave as food. Check your answers in Leviticus 11:1-47 and Deuteronomy 14:1-20.

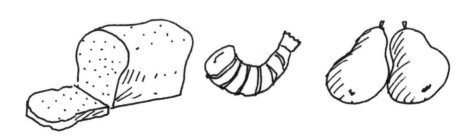

Finding a Healthy Balance

Eating a healthy, balanced diet and having an active lifestyle is very important during puberty. Try to vary your food choices to include all five basic food groups, particularly those rich in calcium (milk, yogurt, and cheese) and iron (meat, beans, and eggs). Below is the newly designed U.S. Food Guide Pyramid to help girls like you know what they should eat and do to stay healthy.

(www.mypyramid.gov)

The pyramid shows food groups as a series of differently sized shaded stripes, each one with different widths showing how much of a girl's daily food intake should be made up of that food group. The criteria are no longer based on the number of servings you eat, but is tied directly to how much you exercise. Girls that are extremely active will need more food for fuel, in addition to growth.

Use the *Girls Calorie Food Chart* to find out what your daily food intake should be. It is based on your age, gender, and how physically active you are during the day. Once you have found your age and activity level, follow the chart across to find out how much you should be eating in each food group. Keep in mind, one size doesn't fit all. This is just an estimate to get you started.

Girls Calorie Food Chart

AGE	*PHYSICAL ACTIVITY	GRAINS	VEGETABLE	FRUITS	MILK	MEAT/BEANS	**DAILY CALORIES
8	< 30 minutes	5 ounces	1.5 cups	1.5 cups	2 cups	4 ounces	1400
8	30 to 60 minutes	5 ounces	2 cups	1.5 cups	3 cups	5 ounces	1600
8	> 60 minutes	6 ounces	2.5 cups	1.5 cups	3 cups	5 ounces	1800
9	< 30 minutes	5 ounces	1.5 cups	1.5 cups	2 cups	4 ounces	1400
9	30 to 60 minutes	6 ounces	2 cups	1.5 cups	3 cups	5 ounces	1600
9	> 60 minutes	6 ounces	2.5 cups	1.5 cups	3 cups	5 ounces	1800
10	< 30 minutes	5 ounces	1.5 cups	1.5 cups	2 cups	4 ounces	1400
10	30 to 60 minutes	6 ounces	2.5 cups	1.5 cups	3 cups	5 ounces	1800
10	> 60 minutes	6 ounces	2.5 cups	2 cups	3 cups	5.5 ounces	2000
11	< 30 minutes	5 ounces	2 cups	1.5 cups	3 cups	5 ounces	1600
11	30 to 60 minutes	6 ounces	2.5 cups	1.5 cups	3 cups	5 ounces	1800
11	> 60 minutes	6 ounces	2.5 cups	2 cups	3 cups	5.5 ounces	2000
12	< 30 minutes	5 ounces	2 cups	1.5 cups	3 cups	5 ounces	1600
12	30 to 60 minutes	6 ounces	2.5 cups	2 cups	3 cups	5.5 ounces	2000
12	> 60 minutes	7 ounces	3 cups	2 cups	3 cups	6 ounces	2200

*Physical Activity: Amount of moderate or vigorous activity (such as brisk walking, jogging, biking, aerobics, or yard work) you do in addition to your normal daily routine every other day.

**This calorie level is only an estimate of your needs. Monitor your body weight to see if you need to adjust your calorie intake.

Comparing Apples to Apples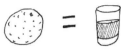

Well, almost. Except in this case it helps to find some common comparisons when determining appropriate serving sizes. Here is an easy-to-remember guide to follow:

BReaDS, GRaiNS (equivalent to 1 ounce)

✳ 1 slice of bread = CD case

✳ 1 pancake or waffle = DVD

✳ 1 bagel = drink coaster

✳ 1 tortilla = 7" dinner plate

Other one ounce equivalents include: 1 cup of ready to eat cereal, ½ cup cooked rice, ½ English muffin, cooked pasta, two oatmeal raisin cookies, or ½ cup cooked oatmeal.

FRuitS (equivalent to 1 cup)

✳ 1 medium apple = tennis ball

✳ ½ cup dried fruit = iPod

Other one-cup equivalents include: 1 medium-size fruit, ½ cup juice.

VeGetaBLeS (equivalent to 1 cup)

✳ 1 medium potato = computer mouse

✳ ½ cup cooked peas = golf ball

✳ 1 small fries = cell phone

Other one cup equivalents include: 1 cup of raw carrot sticks, 1 cup cooked vegetables, or 2 cups of raw dark leafy greens.

MeatS (equivalent to 1 ounce, unless otherwise noted)

✳ 1 hamburger = deck of cards (equivalent to 4 ounces)

✳ 1 tablespoons of peanut butter = ping pong ball

✳ 1 medium egg = well, an egg!

Other one ounce equivalents include, 1 ounce of poultry or fish, ½ cup cooked dry beans, 1 egg, or ½ ounce of nuts or seeds.

Dairy, Cheese (equivalent to 1 ounce)

❄ 1 ounce cheese = 1½ dominoes

❄ 1 cup milk = ice cream cone

Other one cup equivalents include 1 cup yogurt or 2 ounces of processed cheese.

How Do I Count the Oils?

A girl between the ages 9 and 13 years old should only consume 5 teaspoons of oil in her daily diet. This includes oils from fish, fried foods, cooking oil, and salad dressings.

Head-To-Toe Tip

Top Five Healthy Eating Habits

See how you score with these healthy tips on nutrition.

✳ **Eat a variety of foods.** Your daily selection of foods should include bread and other whole-grain products, fruits, vegetables, dairy, meat and poultry proteins.

✳ **Keep portion sizes reasonable.** Don't over do it with super-sizing. Check food labels on packaging for number of servings to avoid overeating.

✳ **Eat regular meals.** Skipping meals can lead to out-of-control hunger and overeating. Don't miss meals as a way of dieting, either.

✳ **Eat snacks** such as carrot sticks, whole wheat crackers, or yogurt between meals to help get you through the afternoon after school or after soccer practice. Just don't let the snack become a substitute for a meal.

✳ **Eat foods in moderation.** No food is good or bad if your nutritional needs are being met. It's okay to have potato chips with your tuna sandwich or pumpkin pie at Thanksgiving.

What's on the Menu?

Here's a chance for you to fill out this menu with all your favorites for one day. One catch though: it has to match your nutritional requirements from the *Girls Calories Food Chart*. (Not all blanks have to be filled.)

TODay'S SPeCialS

Main Entree

_____

_____

_____

Appetizers for Starters

_____

_____

_____

Cold Sandwiches

_____

_____

_____

Hot off the Grill

_____

_____

_____

Soups, Salads, Sides

_____

_____

_____

Eat Your Veggies

_____

_____

_____

Beverages

_____

_____

_____

Desserts

_____

_____

_____

> *Then God said, "I give you every seed-bearing plant on the face of the whole earth and every tree that has fruit with seed in it. They will be yours for food."*   Genesis 1:29

InstaMssg Irene:
Anorexia and Bulimia

Dear Irene:

I have heard in the news a lot lately about Hollywood Stars that have anorexia and bulimia. What exactly is it? I think I have been gaining more weight recently, though my friends say I am as skinny as a rail.

Too Thin

Dear Too Thin:

Anorexia and bulimia are two eating disorders that affect girls who experience a distorted self-image of their body. Everyone sees them as thin, but when they look in the mirror they see someone who is fat. A girl with anorexia will become obsessed with what she eats. She has an intense fear of being fat and will hardly eat any food. It is okay to be conscious about if you are eating healthy and watching your weight. But, it's not healthy to be obsessed with it.

With bulimia, on the other hand, a girl will eat loads of food then get rid of it quickly by vomiting or taking laxatives. This is known as the "binge and purge" behavior. Both are very dangerous conditions. Here are the tell-tale signs to know if you or someone you know may have either of these:

Anorexia

- ✳ loses a lot of weight
- ✳ denies body's hunger pains
- ✳ feels fat
- ✳ quits normal activities to be alone
- ✳ exercise excessively

Bulimia

- ✳ eats large amounts of food
- ✳ uses laxatives
- ✳ makes excuses to use restroom right after meals
- ✳ quits normal activities to be alone

For girls like yourself, it is normal to gain some body weight during puberty. You shouldn't worry too much about what the scales say and be more concerned about eating healthy meals and getting plenty of exercise. Your shape will continue to change and become curvier as time goes by. It's good that you are educating yourself on these disorders. If you need to, talk to another trusted adult like a parent or friend at church who can answer other questions you may have these conditions.

Irene

InstaMssg Irene: Dieting

Dear Irene:

I am 12 years old and weigh about 130 pounds. I don't like the way I look and kids at school are always teasing me. When I went for a checkup, the doctor said I was fine and not to worry about the extra weight because I'll grow into it. I still want to go on a diet to lose the extra weight. What should I do?

Bulging Becky

Dear Bulging Becky:

I have a question for you. What kind of diet are you considering? Are you eating sugared snacks and sweets? Do you eat cereal in the morning loaded down with sugar? Are you having cakes, pies and ice cream frequently after meals? Are you eating foods high in fat, like meat and potatoes with gravy? Really, all you have to do is change your diet by substituting the sweets with fruits and vegetables and eat lean meat at meals and you will be fine.

You also need to include regular exercise. Instead of plopping yourself down in front of the TV or computer when you get home from school, enjoy the rest of the day outside by running, jumping, and playing games with kids in the neighborhood. Your doctor may be right, it will be fine but only if you change your diet and exercise regularly.

Irene

But the LORD said to Samuel, "Do not consider his appearance or his height, for I have rejected him. The LORD does not look at the things man looks at. Man looks at the outward appearance, but the LORD looks at the heart." 1 Samuel 16:7

Vending to Healthy Snacks

Come hungry to this vending machine to find a variety of wholesome snacks. No, you won't find the usual chips, candy bars, or sodas. Our selection is only snacks that are healthy and will give your changing body the energy it needs. Don't forget, today's girls need that winning edge. As always, get adult assistance when cooking.

Protein Energy Bars

Instead of reaching for a candy bar, grab one of these energy bars to get the pickup you need after a game or practice.

What You Will Need:

❊ plastic wrap
❊ plastic container with cover
❊ mixing bowl
❊ blender or knife
❊ spoon
❊ flour
❊ 3 cups dried apples

- ❋ 2 cups dried apricots
- ❋ 1 cup pitted prunes
- ❋ 1 cup pitted dates
- ❋ 1 cup raisins
- ❋ 1 cup sunflower seeds (shelled)
- ❋ ¾ cup creamy peanut butter
- ❋ ½ cup margarine, melted
- ❋ ½ cup honey
- ❋ ¼ cup sesame seeds

What To Do:

1. Chop apples, apricots, prunes, and dates (separately) using either a blender or knife. Place chopped fruit into the mixing bowl.
2. Add raisins, sunflower seeds, peanut butter, melted margarine, honey, and sesame seeds to the mixing bowl.
3. On a clean plate or counter, lightly dust with flour.
4. Using your clean hands mix together. Shape the mixture into small logs and roll in flour.
5. Wrap each log in plastic wrap and store in a covered container. Take these on your next hike or family outing.

Sports Power Drink #1

After a long run, you will need a drink that will replenish the minerals your body needs. Here is a recipe that will give you the same benefits as some of your favorite store-bought sports drinks.

What You Will Need:

- ✳ ½ cup orange juice
- ✳ 9 Tablespoons sugar
- ✳ ⅜ teaspoon salt
- ✳ 2 quarts of water

What To Do:

1. In a pitcher, mix orange juice, water, sugar, and salt. Stir.

2. For a zesty change, try substituting 2 tablespoons of lemon juice for the orange juice. You will get the same benefits of the original recipe.

Remember, the exact proportions aren't as important as having the drink for your long runs.

This drink (per 8 oz serving) will provide you with approximately:

- • 14.4 grams carbohydrate
- • 104 mg sodium
- • 28.4 mg Potassium

Sports Power Drink #2

If you are a flying-trapeze-artist-in-training who loves sports drinks, here is one that won't leave you dangling in mid-air.

What You Will Need:

- ✳ saucepan
- ✳ pitcher

- ❋ spoon
- ❋ 4 cups water
- ❋ 2 ½ cups caffeine-free herbal tea
- ❋ ½ tsp salt
- ❋ ½ cup sugar
- ❋ ½ cup orange juice

What To Do:

1. Follow directions on the box for making herbal tea. Let cool.
2. In a saucepan over medium heat, dissolve sugar and salt in water. Let cool.
3. In a pitcher, mix herbal tea, orange juice, and water together. Chill before serving. Makes 2 quarts.

Hiker's Ultimate Trail Mix

This is one snack you do not want to leave home without. Chocked full of vitamins and minerals — this one is sure to score big with friends and family.

What You Will Need:

- ❋ ½ cup dried cranberries
- ❋ ½ cup yogurt raisins
- ❋ ½ cup pretzel sticks
- ❋ ½ cup dried apple pieces
- ❋ ½ cup sunflower seeds
- ❋ ½ cup cashews
- ❋ ½ cup almonds
- ❋ ½ cup miniature marshmallows

✳ ½ cup chocolate chips or candies (substitute: white chocolate chips)

✳ ½ cup peanut butter chips (you can substitute butterscotch chips if you like)

What To Do:

1. In a large bowl, mix all ingredients together.

2. Store in individual sandwich bags for quick snacks on the go or in a plastic covered container. Yummy and great for long car rides.

3. Try different variations by using butterscotch chips instead of peanut butter chips, white chocolate chips instead of chocolate candies, or goldfish crackers instead of pretzels. The possibilities are endless.

Banana Chips

These crunchy snacks will give you the energy to get through the morning and make it to lunch.

What You Will Need:

✳ plastic container with cover

✳ cookie sheet

✳ non-stick cooking spray

✳ spatula

✳ knife

✳ 2 ripe bananas

What To Do:

1. Preheat oven at 150 degrees farenheit.

2. Spray the cookie sheet with nonstick cooking spray to prevent sticking.

3. Slice bananas into thin rounds. Be sure to cut away and remove any bruises.

4. Place the banana slices on the cookie sheet in a single layer.

5. Cook the slices for 2 hours with the oven door left ajar about 1 inch.

6. Flip the banana slices with the spatula and bake additional 2 hours.

7. To test for doneness, they will be hard and breakable.

8. Store your banana chips in a plastic airtight container.

Granola Munch

Here's a snack you will want to make in advance and have ready for those times when you have the munchies.

What You Will Need:

❋ 1 cookie sheet

❋ 1 saucepan

❋ 1 large mixing bowl

❋ non-stick cooking spray

❋ 2½ cups of oats

❋ ½ cup of honey

❋ ½ cup of sliced almonds

❋ ½ cup of wheat nuts (or wheat germ)

✳ ½ cup of raisins (or dried cranberries)

✳ ¼ cup of vegetable oil

What To Do:

1. Preheat oven to 275 degrees farenheit.
2. Spray the cookie sheet with cooking oil spray.
3. In a large bowl, mix all of the dry ingredients.
4. In a saucepan, combine honey and oil. Stir mixture over low heat until warm.
5. Pour honey mixture into bowl with dry ingredients and blend until well coated.
6. Spread mixture onto the baking sheet and bake for one hour or until brown. Stir occasionally to prevent sticking.

Fruity Delight Smoothie

This delicious smoothie is heavenly because it is low fat.

What You Will Need:

✳ blender

✳ various fruits (bananas, strawberries, or oranges)

✳ 8 oz. skim milk

What To Do:

1. Ahead of time, peel bananas and place in a plastic bag. Store in freezer until ready to use.
2. Pour 8 oz. of skim milk in a blender. Add 1 banana per smoothie.

3.: Blend until smooth. Pour in tall glass and enjoy.

4.: For variety, try adding some of your other favorite fruits such as strawberries, apples, or oranges. Just think of the possibilities!

Celebrating with God Devotion: What's for Dinner?

"Mmmm..." Suzie drew a deep breath. "Smell that delicious food."

"Yeah, I'm starved!" Marisa patted her stomach. "Let's get something to eat."

Sizzling smells wafted through the air, calling the girls' names as they walked through the food court at the mall. Each pointed out the various choices they had then they sat at a table amongst bustling shoppers to decide which style of cuisine would satisy their cravings.

"Well, you could get the green pepper steak, Marisa, since you wanted that earlier," Alexis thought out loud. "I could get a salad, and we can split it. Then maybe later I'll get some soup. How about you, Suzie?"

"I'm gonna get fries and a soda," Suzie rattled off her list. "And maybe ice cream for dessert." She started over to the nearest counter.

"Suzie, wait," Alexis called. "You can't just eat junk food. You have to eat some healthy stuff, too."

"Girls, this is a mall. You can't get great food like this every day. I can get that healthy stuff at home. Friday night is my night." Suzie pulled a wad of bills from her jeans pocket. "Besides, that whole eating healthy thing is for grown ups to worry about." She stepped up to the counter of the Burger Slop Shop to place her order. The other two looked at each other shrugging their shoulders.

After dinner, the three continued their shopping spree. Playfully, the girls ran in between the vendors down the center aisle of the mall.

"Wow! That was fun," Marisa exclaimed. Looking around she asked, "Where's Suzie?"

"I don't know." Alexis glanced behind her. "C'mon, let's go find her."

The pair found Suzie sitting on a bench.

"Suzie, are you alright?" Alexis asked.

"I feel kinda sick." Suzie said, holding her stomach.

Marisa said, "Man, sugar overdose!"

"We said you should have eaten something healthy, but you ate all that junk food."

"You know, Suzie, even though we're young, we still need to take care of our bodies and eat healthy." Alexis sat down next to Suzie. "God gave us these beautiful vessels to use for His service and how can we do His work if we're sick all the time?"

Suzie laughed. "Yeah, I guess you're right. I want God to be able to use me." Suzie jumped up. "Now let's go find those bargains!"

You may think that while you are young, you don't have to be concerned about nutrition. But in reality, God does expect you to make healthy choices and take care of your temple. That doesn't mean you need to go overboard and count calories or worry about what kinds of foods that you eat all the time. 1 Corinthians 8:8 tells us, "But food does not bring us near to God; we are no worse if we do not eat, and no better if we do." In other words, it's not what you eat that makes you a better Christian, but feeding your body what it needs will enable you to have a better relationship with God. He has big plans for you, so eat healthy.

QUICK Quiz

Unsweetened or Sugar-hol-ic?

Do you have a sweet tooth or are you a closet sugar-hol-ic who needs a quick fix — morning, noon and night? Take this short quiz to find out if you are consuming too much sugar.

1. HOW OFTEN DO YOU EAT PRE-SWEETENED CEREAL?

A. never   B. 1 or 2 times a week

C. once a day   D. three or more a day

2. HOW OFTEN DO YOU DRINK SODAS, FRUIT DRINK

BOXES, PUNCH, OR OTHER SWEETENED DRINKS?

A. never   B. 1 or 2 times a week

C. once a day   D. three or more a day

3. HOW OFTEN DO YOU EAT CANDY OR SWEETS WITH SUGAR IN THEM?

A. never   B. 1 or 2 times a week

C. once a day   D. three or more a day

4. HOW OFTEN DO YOU EAT COOKIES, SNACK CAKES, BROWNIES, ETC.?

A. never   B. 1 or 2 times a week

C. once a day   D. three or more a day

Did you circle 1 or 2 times a week for most of your answers? Or, are you over-the-top and eating sugar three or more times a day? If so, you will want to think about how much sugar you are consuming and try to cut back on the white stuff. The less you eat, the less your body will crave it.

Sugar Buzz—The Real Story Behind the Sweet Stuff

Sugar gives you a surge of energy, but a short time later you're tired and suddenly craving more. That's because when the sugar hits your bloodstream your pancreas releases a hormone called insulin, which carries sugar to your liver. Your liver goes into overdrive to get rid of the extra blood ugar, zapping your energy. You end up crashing, feeling tired, cranky, nd sick. Ugh!

"Therefore I tell you, do not worry about your life, what you will eat or drink; or about your body, what you will wear. Is not life more important than food, and the body more impor-tant than clothes? Look at the birds of the air; they do not sow or reap or store away in barns, and yet your heavenly Father feeds them. Are you not much more valuable than they?"

Matthew 6:25-26

Try This:

Describe a time when you felt a little **DEVILISH** and caved in to a craving temptation. How did God help you overcome it?

Chapter Nine

My Soul: Warm Fuzzy Feelings & All

As a father has compassion on his children, so the LORD has compassion on those who fear him; for he knows how we are formed, he remembers that we are dust.

~Psalm 103:13-14

SiNCe ENTeRiNG PUBeRTY HaS LiFe SUDDeNLY GOTTeN HaRD? Do you feel like you're getting bumped around by your emotions? One minute you're ecstatic, the next minute you're depressed and feel yourself falling into a black hole?

No, you're not losing your mind! It's perfectly normal for girls to experience changes in their emotions as their bodies go through major changes. In this section, you will learn more about the good, the bad, and the ugly of your feelings and steps you can take to manage stress and mood swings.

Feelings, Nothing More Than Feelings

It's true that your feelings will impact the way you think and act. Most of the time, you're probably not even aware of your feelings. At other times, you might experience strong feelings that catch your attention like a romantic crush on a really cute guy at school, or deep sadness when Rover, your best dog, decides to leave home.

Ok, so feelings are those funny sensations you get in your body. Every girl (and guy) has them. They do seem to get stronger during puberty, however. But, you may not always understand them. Some people will try to tell you, **"YOU SHOULDN'T FeeL THaT WaY!"** That's not right. You have a right to feel any emotion because feelings aren't good or bad. They're just feelings.

FeeLiNGS aRe a CHOiCe. No one can make you feel a certain way. They're yours. If someone says something mean to you, you decide whether to get mad, sad, etc. It's up to you how to react. Are you going to become angry and scream back? Or, will you ignore them and stay cool? This is how you can learn to stay in control of yourself.

Your feelings are there to protect you and help you make wise choices. For instance, you just climbed into bed, when you suddenly saw a large furry spider dangling over your bed. Your brain takes this information straight to the feelings headquarters and flashes, "RUN FOR YOUR LIFE!" You felt scared because danger was near and you reacted quickly.

FeeLiNGS WiLL CHaNGe QUiCKLY, too. After you
take on this eight-legged creature and splatter the poor spider's guts all over your bedroom wall with a broom, you feel relieved. Your "scared" feeling is now replaced with another feeling: relief. You know, "Whew, that was a close one, folks," kind of feeling.

YOUR feeLiNGS COMe iN DiffereNt SHaPeS aND SiZeS. Some of them may be unique to you. For instance, the
feeling you had in your stomach after eating your latest creation: peanut butter layered with sardines and pickles on rye. But let's just talk about the most common feelings that we've all had, at one time or another.

How Do You Feel?

With all the changes going on inside your body, a variety of feelings come with it. (Blame the hormones.) Check out this list of feelings. How many of these have you already experienced this week? Circle all that apply.

disgusted	bored	confused
guilty	anticipation	nervous
happy	sad	lonely

frightened	love struck	exhausted
angry	smug	overwhelmed
hopeful	shy	anxious
mischievous	ecstatic	embarrassed
jealous	frustrated	depressed
surprised	proud	smart

Pampered by The WORD

A happy heart makes the face cheerful, but heartache crushes the spirit.
Proverbs 15:13

Roller Coaster Days

How many feelings did you circle? Did you circle a lot of diametrically opposed feelings (opposite from each other)? The ups and downs of emotions you experienced are called "mood swings." But, not to worry. It is all part of the package of growing up.

Keep in mind, just because your emotions may make you feel a bit out of control, that doesn't give you a license to sin or go out and do something you will regret later. You are still responsible for your actions. For instance, you're upset and feel angry because you didn't win a contest at school. That's okay. But, if you come home and kick your cat because you're still sore about losing, that's not okay.

It's what you do with your feelings that's important. That's why understanding your feelings will help you deal with the problem at hand without hurting yourself or someone else.

More Than a Feeling

As you change, you are probably going to want to spend more time with your friends hanging out than at home with the family. That's part of becoming self-sufficient and your own person. You may want to spend more time in your room alone, or talking on the phone with a girlfriend. This time may be a bit awkward for you and your family. You will want to be more independent and to start making decisions for yourself, while your family may still want to treat you like a six-year-old. Try not to let this get to you. Instead, plan time for both friends and family. Of course, make sure you have time for yourself and time with God, too. Nothing's more important than that.

You may already feel a bit self-conscious (okay, a lot) about your parents and the way they act. At the mall, you walk at least twenty feet ahead of them, hoping no one will mistakenly think you are with them. Or, Dad picks you up at school wearing his Scottish Kilt on his way home from an American-Scottish meeting. What was he thinking? Or, doesn't Mom have any clue the minivan with three missing hub-

165

caps and a taped-up plastic window is a total embarrassment to the family name? How could she?

You feel embarrassed and don't want to be seen with your dweeby parents because you are not a kid anymore and are now realizing they aren't the super heroes you once thought they were. Again, this is not something to fret about. All girls going through puberty are experiencing the same thing. No one is going to judge you because of your parents' behavior. (Your friends will be too worried thinking about their own parents.)

Don't get caught up in what your friends think and then cave in to the pressure of doing something you know is wrong, just to be a part of the crowd. **Stick to your beliefs and be your own person!** God will be there to strengthen you and get you through it if you let Him.

And finally, now that you are becoming a lady, you will want to have more privacy. It's okay to want to change in your bedroom with the door closed and need privacy while showering, etc. You may even be modest with your girlfriends in the locker room. That's all part of becoming a woman. If at any time someone touches you in a way that is not appropriate or makes you uncomfortable, tell an adult as soon as possible. Never try to protect the person who is hurting you. It's your body and God's temple — protect it.

All of these emotional changes are a part of life, so hang on for the ride! If this part of the roller coaster ride makes you sick, hang in there. It will be over soon. If you are amused with it, then throw your hands in the air and give thanks to God because before you know it, the ride will be over.

Head-To-Toe Tip

What Do You Know About Pressure?

Wash the dishes! Take out the trash! Do your homework! Pressure can sometimes feel overwhelming. Do you sometimes feel like falling back into the nearest chair with your arms and legs spread out? Would eight arms like an octopus come in handy right now? Pressure is all a part of growing up. Here are some hints on how to manage it better.

✳ Set priorities. Spend your time on what's really important. Don't waste time on projects that are unrelated to your goals.

✳ Know what works for you. Are you distracted by the TV when you're trying to get a book report done? Or, do you study better at the library? Find out what motivates you so you'll get your work done.

✳ Make a schedule. Instead of waiting until the night before to write your term paper, try organizing your time with an appointment book. Have a set time each day for working on a project and other studies, like early morning before school.

✳ Write it down. Instead of keeping track of every to-do in your mind, give it a rest by keeping track on paper. You will feel relief when you can scratch it off your list.

Express Yourself

Expressing your feelings on paper helps to relieve stress and tension and to get in touch with your emotions. It also helps you better understand what's going on inside you. Answer these five questions below, to help you better identify your feelings.

1. Describe a time when you felt disgusted. How did God help you through it?

2. Draw a picture of what you look like when you feel bored. What do you do to keep from feeling bored?

3. When was the last time you felt confused? What happened?

4. List five things that make you ecstatic. What do you do when you feel ecstatic?

5. Write about a time when guilty feelings made you turn yourself in and confess your sin. How did God help you through it?

Your BFF's Interview

Here's your chance to be a roving reporter and get the scoop on your best friend's feelings. Take the next ten minutes to interview your best buddy and find out how she manages her emotions. Her answers might surprise you. This will be a great way to get to know one another better.

1. What do you look forward to doing? How do you hope God will use you someday?

2. Describe a time when you felt nervous about something. Did you pray or sing a song? How did God help you through it?

3. Write about the most embarrassing moment of your life. Is it funny now, looking back? How has God used this situation in your life to teach you?

4. How has God blessed you and made you happy? Write as many blessings as you can think of here.

5. Do you ever feel sad? What do you do to cheer yourself up? List all the ways you try to make yourself feel better.

Insta MSSG   InstaMssg Irene: Vision of Love

Dear Irene:

The dreamiest guy in my science class sits in front of me. Once he turned around to borrow a pencil and I could hardly speak, my

heart was beating so fast. I sat there staring at him, so he turned to the boy across the aisle and got a pencil from him. Is this what love feels like?

Vision of Love

Dear Vision of Love:

It can sometimes be tough to tell the difference between a crush or "puppy love" and real love. Time always tells, though. Crushes are short-lived, with a lot of physical reactions. For instance, you may get nervous around this guy and your heart beats really fast in your chest. Or, you feel like you've got butterflies in your stomach. Real love involves more than just feelings. It's spending time with the person and getting to know them. You will also grow to respect them and care for them. Love can start out this way, but it evolves into something much deeper. Feelings may not always be there when you love someone, but your commitment to that person, regardless of how you feel, should be.

Irene

Fill-in Prayer: Feelings

God, my emotions have been like a roller coaster lately. One minute I am happy, the next minute sad. Sometimes, I try to hide my feelings from others, but I know You see everything and know the way I feel inside. Thank You that I can come with boldness and share my heart with You.

Today, I am feeling _____ because

_____

_____

_____. Please help me through this time.

In Jesus' name, Amen.

All my _____ lie open before you, O Lord; my _____ is not _____ from you. *Psalm 38:9*

Make IT! Rainbow Twirl Lip Gloss

Here's a wonderful treat for the "smackers."
Have fun trying different combinations like
strawberry/banana, cherry/vanilla, and chocolate/peppermint.

What You Will Need:

✳ saucepan

✳ grater

✳ 1 teaspoon beeswax (available at your health food store)

✳ 1 teaspoon petroleum jelly

✳ ½ teaspoon un-medicated aloe vera gel

✳ ½ teaspoon apricot kernel oil

✳ ¼ teaspoon grated crayon (any color combination of
children's non-toxic crayons)

✳ 3 drops of flavoring (available at the grocery store
or cake decorating store) OR

✳ flavored powdered drink mix

What To Do:

1. Melt the beeswax and crayons in a
saucepan, then remove from heat.

2. Add the petroleum jelly and aloe
vera gel right away.

3. Stir for a couple of minutes until
completely dissolved.

4. Add the apricot kernel oil and 3
drops of flavoring or flavored powdered drink mix and stir for another
minute.

5: Pour lip gloss mixture into small containers or pots. Use anytime for that winning smile.

Finally, brothers, whatever is true, whatever is noble, whatever is right, whatever is pure, whatever is lovely, whatever is admirable – if anything is excellent or praiseworthy -- think about such things. Whatever you have learned or received or heard from me, or seen in me – put it into practice. And the God of peace will be with you.

Philippians 4:8-9

Celebrating with God Devotion: Horror Movie Dilemma

Exhausted, the girls rested for a minute on a bench after spending almost an hour in line for the opening night of the hottest new movie, "Ice Princess." Marisa and Suzie ran off to take a restroom break, while Alexis sat waiting for the two girls. Alexis studied the movie posters in the lobby around her, searching for the new shows they could see next weekend. Suddenly, she heard her named called. Alexis looked up expecting to see her friends, but instead saw Claire — one of the most popular girls in her class — with her cheerleader friends. Alexis braced herself when they sauntered over with their noses in the air.

"Hey Alexis, what are you doing here?" Claire put her hands on her hips. "Don't you have a Barbie at your Malibu palace that needs an outfit change?"

"Yeah, where are your parents? Or that purple dinosaur that baby-sits you in the afternoon?" Claire's friends chimed in mocking her.

Alexis nervously pushed a strand of sandy blonde hair behind her ear. "I'm here with my friends. And Suzie's parents said we could see the new animated movie by ourselves."

"Really, now?" Claire bent her tall frame down to Alexis' level. "If you're so grown up now, why do you come with us to see the 'Fires of Hell' horror flick?"

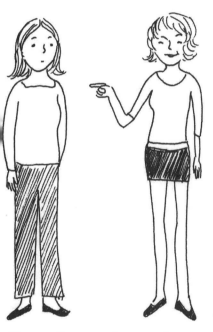

"Afraid of a little fire, Scarecrow?" Claire's friends whined.

Alexis frowned. She had always wanted to be in the popular group at school with all the pretty, talented cheerleaders. If she went with them to see the horror movie, Claire would think she was cool. But she knew her parents wouldn't like it and God wouldn't want her to watch something that glorified evil.

"I'm not afraid..." Alexis quickly responded.

She really wasn't scared to go in and thought to do it just to prove them wrong. Just then, Marisa and Suzie returned, making their way to her side.

"Oh, your loser friends are here now. Will they be coming with us?" Claire sneered.

"Well, I- I mean, we-" Alexis stuttered.

"Coming where?" Suzie questioned.

"To watch the horror movie, that's where," Claire's friend replied.

"We're not going with you losers to watch some horror movie," Marisa interjected.

"Our parents don't want us going in there, and God doesn't like it, either." Suzie said, turning to Alexis. "C'mon, let's go watch the movie we came to see."

After Claire and her friends stomped off, Alexis smiled sadly at her friends.

"Thanks, guys. I almost went with them." She sighed. "I knew what the right thing to do was, but I wanted to be popular, like Claire."

Suzie grinned at Alexis. "You don't need to be in their group. They're a bunch of stuck-up snobs. It doesn't matter what they think. It's much better to be popular with God, because it is only His opinion that really matters."

Have you ever been pressured to do something you know is wrong? The pressure to be popular can be really tough. Cool people at school may try to get you to do things you know aren't right and you may feel like you have to in order to be a part of their group. But that isn't cool at all. What is cool is doing what is right. When you do, others may not agree with your choice, but God cares, and it pleases Him. You'll be in His group of popular friends, and that's what really matters.

Try This:

What frightens you? **A SCaRY MOVIe?** Shadows on the walls at night? Draw a picture of what makes you feel this way. How does God help you when you feel frightened?

Chapter Ten

My Spirit: Soaring with God

But those who hope in the LORD will renew their strength. They will soar on wings like eagles; they will run and not grow weary, they will walk and not be faint.
~Isaiah 40:31

BY NOW, YOU KNOW THE IMPORTANCE OF TAKING CARE OF YOUR BODY — GOD'S TEMPLE. However, your outside shell isn't all there is. Your spirit and the essence of who you are is the real you. Even if you see yourself as "plain Jane," you are still beautiful because real beauty comes from a heart that radiates the love of Jesus. This doesn't mean you have to love every feature about yourself, like your complexion or hair color. Most girls don't. But, you are blessed with so much more than physical appearance, like hopes and dreams for your future, ambition to fulfill the visions God has placed in your heart, and special gifts He gave you to use. You are uniquely you!

Try This:

Name five things you can do to **LIFT YOUR SPIRITS.** Now, write down a favorite scripture you can memorize. Say it aloud when you begin to feel gloomy.

1.

2.

3.

4.

5.

Beauty Isn't Skin Deep

Think about your best friend for a minute. How would you describe her? Circle all the words below that describe her personality. Now, do it again using a different color pen and circle all the words that describe you.

ARTISTIC	friendly	KIND	funny
HELPFUL	*light-hearted*	**honest**	*warm*
comical	*athletic*	curious	enthusiastic
creative	honorable	**witty**	*loving*
imaginative	clever	patient	**cheerful**
accepting	**silly**	playful	*compassionate*
forgiving	humble	inspiring	**supportive**
OPTIMISTIC	open-minded	encouraging	*trustworthy*
good-looking	ENERGETIC	original	LEADER

As you can see by your circles for your friend, it's not really important what she looks like. You like her for who she is and, you have a lot of good qualities your friends like about you too. These things are what make you special, and with God, you are becoming the woman He desires you to be.

179

Role Model

You may know of some women in your life that you look up to as a role model, such as a parent or teacher. Or, maybe it's a star athlete or famous author you admire. Think about why you admire and respect them. Are these qualities you have or would like to have? You can use the qualities you do have to be the best you can be in whatever you do. Everything you do today can improve your life. It's about looking in the mirror at yourself and liking what you see.

Kerri Strug, a 1996 Olympic Gold medalist in womens gymnastics said, "The courage to soar to great heights is inside all of us." She's right. **GOD WaNts you to soaR, But it's UP to you!**

Stop now and take a look at yourself in the mirror and read this to the girl staring back at you:

> *"I am a wonderful person that God created. I am beautiful on the inside and out. I can expect good things to happen to me. I am a good friend and don't judge others by the way they look. I can do all things with Jesus' help and will be successful in all my plans and accomplish my goals. I take very good care of my body and feel great. I will feed my body both physically with food and spiritually with the Word of God. I will run the race to win for Christ and remember to exercise every day to take care of God's temple. He loves me no matter what and I love Him."*

These words aren't a magic potion or spell. It will be up to you to take action to improve your body with what you've learned in this book and accept the responsibility for the choices you make in diet, personal care, and fitness. Being an active participant in your own future is what will empower you with confidence to spread your wings and fly.

Anyone who listens to the word but does not do what it says is like a man who looks at his face in a mirror and, after looking at himself, goes away and immediately forgets what he looks like. But the man who looks intently into the perfect law that gives freedom, and continues to do this, not forgetting what he has heard, but doing it — he will be blessed in what he does.
James 1:23-25

Prayer: My Future

Dear God,

You were the one who created me and I thank You for making me unique with lots of special qualities. The Scriptures say You knitted me together in my mother's womb. I think that is awesome that You know me inside and out. I am looking forward to the future and the course You have set for me. Teach me to do Your will and guide me in each step. In Jesus' name, Amen.

I will _____ you and _____ you in the _____ you

should _____; I will _____ you and _____ over you.

Psalm 32:8

Head-To-Toe Tip

Soaring as a New Creation

It's true that when you came to know Jesus as your savior, you become a new creation. You were born anew! Now, just like the personal care you do for your skin and nails, your spirit needs care so that you will grow and mature into a Godly woman. Listed below is a daily regimen to keep you spiritually fit:

※ Read God's word daily.

※ Set aside 15 minutes a day to be with God alone.

※ Pray and listen to God. He will

※ listen and speak to you.

※ Keep a journal of these special times with God.

※ Surround yourself with friends who share your faith.

※ Treat others with respect regardless of the way they look. You know that it's what is on the inside that matters most.

Now, you're ready to fly!

InstaMssg Irene:
Messy Friendship

Dear Irene:

My family and I are Messianic Jews. This year I started attending a Christian school near my house. Even though many of my family's beliefs are the same as my Christian friends, there are some differences, like we keep Torah and worship on Sabbath (Friday eve to Saturday eve). Some of my friends at school tease me about the way we do things. I don't seem to fit in and they are always ganging up on me. I do believe in Jesus (Yeshua) the Messiah. What can I do?

Bessy Believes

Dear Bessy Believes:

Your uniqueness as one of "God's chosen" is a special thing that is easily misunderstood. Remind your friends that Jesus was Jewish and your family is just doing what Jesus did when He was here 2,000 years ago. For instance, He kept the Feast of Tabernacles in John 7:2 and Feast of Passover in John 2:23. See if your parents will let you invite your friends over on Sabbath (Friday eve at sundown). You can show them how your tradition of lighting the Sabbath candles with the prayer over the bread and wine is what Yeshua did at the Last Supper. I believe this will give your friends a deeper appreciation for the

Scriptures and respect for your faith in Him. Their lack of understanding in your beliefs is one of the reasons we have so many denominations today. But, Jesus' last prayer to the Father in the garden was that we would be one as He and the Father are one. No matter what our race, skin color, or denomination is, believers are all one in the Messiah.

Irene

Therefore, if anyone is in Christ, he is a new creation; the old has gone, the new has come!

2 Corinthians 5:17

Grounded or Ready for Take Off?

Hopefully by this time you are soaring with God and are putting some of the ideas presented in this book into practice. Take this quiz as your final send off. Check off those statements that describe you:

_____ Listen to your body and know when it's hungry, thirsty, or needs rest.

_____ Comfortable with the changes going on inside and loving it.

_____ Understand the merry-go-round of menstruation and ready for it.

_____ Realize feelings are just feelings and don't let them control you.

_____ Follow a skin and hair care regimen and take care of your nails weekly.

_____ Exercise regularly and feel great.

_____ Use the workout log to set fitness goals.

____ Eating a healthy, well-balanced diet when possible.

____ Spend time with God every day praying and reading your Bible.

____ Don't judge others by their looks and respect everyone.

____ Keep a journal of all the wonderful things happening to you.

____ Happy to be the way God made you.

Soaring With God Journal

Your body has changed in many ways this year. List here some of the changes and how you feel about your body:

_____

_____

_____

_____

Some of the ways you need to take better care of yourself are:

_____

_____

_____

Things you have learned to accept about your-self with God's help:

_____

_____

_____

 **Quick Quiz**

Christian Teen Magazine

Here's your latest issue of *Christian Teen*. Scan the table of contents to see what's inside the magazine. Fill in the blanks below to find the articles for the questions below:

1. To read how one woman's problems with her menstrual period was healed, you would turn to _____.

2. To learn more beauty secrets, you would turn to _____.

3. To read about new fashion colors, you would turn to _____.

4. If you wanted to read about how to dress with modesty, you would turn to _____.

5. To learn about taking a power walk on the Capernaum Sea, you would turn to _____.

6. If you wanted to learn about what to do with leftovers, you would turn to _____.

7. To read about new hair styles and lengths, you would turn to _____.

8. To read about feeding a hungry crowd, you would turn to _____.

9. To learn how to make things taste great using seasonings, you would turn to _____.

10. If you wanted to learn about money matters, you would turn to _____.

BEAUTY

Hair . . . . 1 Cor. 6:6 -15
New looks, new lengths

Tips for Glowing Complexion. 75

Perfect 10 Hands 52

RELAX & HAVE FUN

...eep . . . . Psalm 44:23
...oes God Snooze?

...ecipes to Collect 20
...ody Glitter

FEATURES

HEALTH / FITNESS

FASHION

Celebrating with God Devotion: Soaring with God

The sun laid low in the autumn sky as the first star appeared with a few sherbet-colored clouds dotting the horizon. Neon lights flickered on then flashed in beat to the music on all the midway rides as the sun began to set. Vendors sold glow-in-the-dark necklaces as they wove their way through the lines. Alexis, Suzie, and Marisa joined Suzie's parents at their assigned meeting place and together rode on the giant Ferris wheel before starting home. As they headed toward the gates, Suzie spotted the Hang Gliders.

"Oh, Mom! Look!" Suzie clapped her hands. "I love that ride. Can we go on it, please?"

"It's getting late, sweetie," Mrs. Park answered. "We have to go to church tomorrow."

"Yes, we have to get your friends home, too," Mr. Park added.

"But it's my favorite ride. This is the last one, I promise!" Suzie pleaded.

"Alright. Your dad and I will be at this bench waiting." Mrs. Park sat down. "We have to leave right after this one, okay?"

"Oh, thanks!" Suzie ran to get in line with Alexis and Marisa tagging along. They excitedly chatted about all the rides they had gone on that day while they waited.

But, as the girls got closer to the ride's entrance, Alexis began to worry.

"Wow, look how high it goes!" Marisa pointed at the screaming riders.

"Um, I don't know. Maybe I should sit this one out," Alexis said with uncertainty.

"Aw, c'mon, Alexis," Suzie patted her friend's back. "I've been on it before. It's really fun!"

"Yeah, just try it," Marisa encouraged. "Don't worry, it's my first time, too."

Alexis continued to explain her concerns, but the other two wouldn't hear it. They handed the attendant their tickets and tugged her through the gate.

All of the girls squealed with delight during the ride. Afterwards, they ran to join Suzie's parents.

"That was so fun!" Marisa exclaimed.

"I love that ride," Suzie said, turning to Alexis. "Aren't you glad you tried it?"

"Yeah, that was great!" Alexis said. "I think it was the best one we rode all day."

On their way home in the Park family's green minivan, the three girls discussed all of their favorite rides. Suzie's parents listened quietly in the front, then Mrs. Park piped up.

"You know girls, each of those rides you went on is like a part of your life," she said.

The three thought for a moment, then agreed with her.

"I guess the glasshouse is like how magazines and television try to make us think we're too fat or short when we're actually just perfect the way we are," Suzie started.

"Yeah, and the roller coaster is like our changing emotions, how we can be happy one minute and crying the next," Marisa chimed in.

Alexis smiled. "And the hang gliders are like our relationship with God. It can be scary at first, but once we take that step of faith and trust that it'll be all right, we will by soaring with Him. And, with God, it is the most exciting and exhilarating ride of your life!"

✳ ✳ ✳ ✳ ✳ ✳ ✳ ✳ ✳ ✳ ✳ ✳ ✳ ✳ ✳ ✳ ✳ ✳ ✳ ✳
✳

Have you ever thought about how rides at an amusement park are like events in your life? Maybe there are days when you can't get your hair to stay put and it flies around like the big swings. Or, maybe your menstrual cycle feels like a carousel with your emotions up one week and down the next. All these wonderful changes going on in your body (inside and out) may be a little scary like riding the free fall. But God will get you through them all and as you know, when God is the center of your life, you can always expect life will be just as exciting!

✳ ✳ ✳ ✳ ✳ ✳ ✳ ✳ ✳ ✳ ✳ ✳ ✳ ✳ ✳ ✳ ✳ ✳ ✳ ✳

Try This:

✳

List your hopes and dreams.

How will God help you achieve them?

_____

_____

_____

_____

_____